4

The Great Drought of 1976

The Great Drought of 1976

Evelyn Cox

Hutchinson of London

Hutchinson & Co. (Publishers) Ltd
3 Fitzroy Square, London W I P 6 J D

London Melbourne Sydney Auckland
Wellington Johannesburg and agencies
throughout the world

First published 1978
© Evelyn Cox 1978

Set in Monotype Garamond

Printed in Great Britain by The Anchor Press Ltd
and bound by Wm Brendon & Son Ltd
both of Tiptree, Essex

British Library CIP data

ISBN 0 09 133200 1

Contents

Author's note

This is a factual account of the Great Drought of 1975–6, as experienced on our Herefordshire farm. All the events in it took place. You will not, however, find the village of Micklebury on the map, nor will you find people bearing the names I have used. A community, like an individual, is entitled to its privacy. To preserve that I have not described actual individuals in our locality but have created a series of characters who do not portray any living men and women but do, I believe, reflect truthfully the type of people who shared with us the experience of the drought.

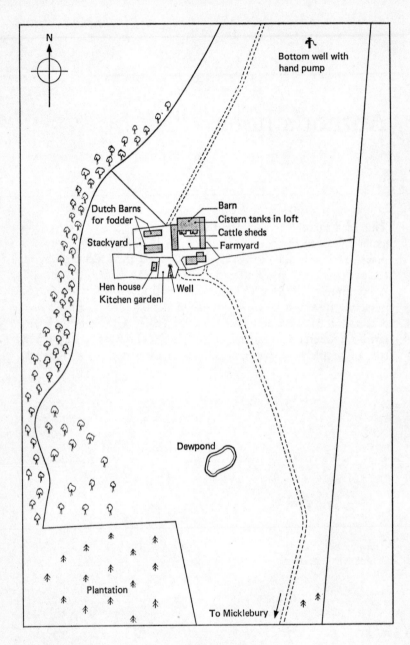

N

Bottom well with hand pump

Dutch Barns for fodder
Barn
Cistern tanks in loft
Cattle sheds
Stackyard
Farmyard
Hen house
Well
Kitchen garden

Dewpond

Plantation

To Micklebury

Map of the farm at Micklebury, Herefordshire

Introduction

In the summer of 1976 Britain had a glimpse of doomsday. Over wide areas of the land one of the elements essential to life, water, became dangerously short. The driest summer for over 200 years showed how vulnerable our crowded and complicated civilization is to such sudden basic changes.

The drought was an experience which divided us into two nations – those whose lives were deeply, and at times dangerously disrupted, and those to whom the drought was at most an over-publicized inconvenience. Nowhere were the effects of this shortage of water more sharply felt than in those rural areas where people – and animals – were dependent directly, not upon regulated supplies from the mains, but upon wells, streams and ponds. For many of these the drought was not a matter of a few summer months, but of a fifteen-month siege.

I experienced that siege, on a Herefordshire farm. I have written down what happened to us, and how we reacted in those long dry months, as this problem thrust itself into every corner of our lives. The drought provided, for those caught up in it, a common, shared experience unlike any other in Britain since the blitz. What we learnt in it may be of some value if another such dry spell hits us. If we are spared such a second ordeal I hope it will be useful to have an immediate record of what the drought was like, before we begin to forget it or before – which is more probable – we begin to embroider our memories into myths.

This therefore is an account of how one Herefordshire farming family survived that waterless year.

1. Forewarning

The drought began for us on 15 October 1975. On that day the dry summer – it had been the hottest of the century so far – finally and inevitably hit our water supplies. The twenty-five-foot deep well that served the farmhouse and buildings was all but dry. In normal times it supplies several hundred gallons of water a day; now it was down to twenty gallons a day. That was enough for the basic needs of the house and an occasional bath, but not for the great family water-consuming activities like washing clothes and flushing the lavatory, let alone for the needs of the livestock. Though we did not know it then, the siege had begun.

Water from the mains was a long-forgotten dream. Our forty-acre farm lies three-quarters of a mile from the nearest road up a rough track. Over the centuries the tide of civilization has ebbed away leaving our farm beached as an isolated settlement amidst the fields and woods of the country of the Marches. Once it was near the hub of the community. The first 350 yards of our track is part of a relief road built by the Romans between the camps they established in the area to keep the Welsh at bay. In some places the Roman paving stones can still be seen but most people driving through the village of Micklebury never guess that this narrow, overgrown lane is still used. The locals call it Rock Bottom Lane because of its foundations – or perhaps because of the state of the finances of the people who use it to reach their homes. In other places it is known as the Micklebury Motorway.

Our own drive branches off this lane and has its own history. It was one of the ancient ridgeways. There is a circle of five pine trees just inside our gate which was originally planted to mark the track on the horizon.

Yet our farm is not quite at the back of beyond. At the end of the track lies the scattered village of Micklebury with its post office and its black and white pub, the Fox and Pheasant. And the nearest market town is only three miles or ten minutes away. But we were well away from the local water mains, and it would have cost the best part of £1000 to connect the farm to the nearest piped supply. We did not have anything like that sum of money to spare. Livestock farming was not lucrative enough for us to raise a loan that would have no immediate effect on productivity.

Then there were engineering problems. As the farm is 460 feet up, the pressure in the mains supply in Micklebury was not high enough to push the water up to us.

Before moving to the farm both my husband, Tom, and I had taken for granted what we now regard as the most basic and underrated of all amenities – a reliable supply of pure water. Before we married I had been a journalist in London and had lived in various flats where water gushed out of taps when they were turned on and sometimes dripped out of them even when they were turned off.

Tom's background was completely different to mine, but he had never had to worry about water shortages either. He was a show-jumping rider specializing in training young horses. In the various stable yards he had occupied, water poured out of taps just as readily as it had done in my various London flats. Before we met he had already started to branch out of the horse business and was keeping cattle on a small holding in Gloucestershire. From that he branched out into more general livestock farming.

In fact Tom's only unfortunate experience with water before the move to Herefordshire was when there had been too much of it. In Gloucestershire, during a dry spell in 1973, we had marvelled at how green the village cricket pitch remained. It was right in front of the house on a strip of common land that separated the farm from the council road. As we looked at the trim oasis of the pitch in the desert of burnt turf we would nod our heads in admiration: 'Wonderful how these old boys keep the wicket in such good order.' Then the rain came and Tom received a telephone call from an agitated chairman of the parish council. 'Please get your fractured water pipe mended. It's waterlogging our cricket pitch and we've got an important match on Saturday.' The pipe from the water main along the road that ran three feet under the common across to the farm had been leaking onto the pitch for weeks. Tom's water demand that summer was three times as high as usual.

We moved farms later that year because the owner of Tom's small holding wanted possession. We chose Herefordshire because the land there was relatively cheap and because we wanted a quiet, peaceful life.

Until the autumn of 1975 we were only too thankful to forego a quarterly water demand. We make a living, but only just, by running a herd of forty beef cattle and a flock of sixty ewes. That year, though, the land had turned sour from carrying too many sheep for too long and we had decided to sell all the sheep and concentrate on cattle.

As well as livestock farming we are also in the horse business. We own a dozen or so horses which my husband trains to go show jumping and we also take horses at livery for breaking and schooling.

The stock and the family – my husband Tom, myself, and our four-month-old baby – and six assorted dogs had to (and we still have to) depend on three sources of natural water. Most comes from the deep well in the vegetable garden by the farmhouse. The water was originally pumped by a picturesque windmill which still stands, or rather leans at an angle of sixty degrees. We have left this landmark intact largely because we have yet to discover how to demolish it without wrecking the well beneath it. But the windmill has been made redundant by an electrically driven pump which draws up the water and pumps it into two 1000-gallon cisterns in the loft of the barn. From there it is piped to the house, the farm buildings and the water troughs in the fields. So once the well runs dry not only the house but most of the farm is without water.

There is a second well in the pasture to the north of the farmhouse but this is more of a nineteenth-century affair. No electric pump here, only one of those antique cast-iron ones with a handle to attach to a human dynamo. To extract water from it is pure hard work. And it is not a good well. After ten days of furious pumping it runs dry.

To the south of the house, almost hidden by the ridge and furrow pattern of the pasture, is a dew-pond. Pools of this type have their origins in prehistory. They are mainly found on the

Sussex Downs and were first constructed to accumulate and store water in areas where there were no other supplies of river or underground water. Built on ridges, they are made by an ancient method using straw and compacted mud to line them. By some miraculous process they do not lose by evaporation during the day the water they gain from the dew nightly.

While there is some doubt about the authenticity of our pond – about whether it was fed by a spring as well as by dew – there is none about its water-retaining ability. About fifteen years ago it did dry up and the tenant of the farm took the opportunity to enlarge it. It refilled naturally, which proper dew-ponds are not supposed to do, and from then on the level changed little from one season to the next.

Like many farms not connected to mains water, ours is ringed with tanks to collect water off the roofs of the house and buildings. With a heavy thunderstorm these tanks can collect over a thousand gallons. The water is used for the stock and, in desperate circumstances, for everything in the house except drinking.

For fifty years these somewhat Heath-Robinson-like arrangements proved adequate to supply the family living at the farm and all the stock on the grounds, which in those days stretched to 200 acres. The deep well had never run dry in living memory and it rained often enough for plenty of water to collect in the rainwater tanks.

But when we moved to the farm in October 1973 there were already the first signs of a possible drought. Ironically water is something Herefordshire is famous for. The county is known for its three 'Ws' – wood, wool and water. It still has its thousands of acres of oak trees, but the famous 'Leominster ore' sheep are extinct. And by the autumn of 1973 signs of danger to the third 'W' had emerged. Several dry winters in succession had begun to affect its extensive underground water supplies.

We had only been on the farm a few weeks before we had a foretaste of what lay ahead. As the autumn of 1973 got under way we discovered that the main well had barely a foot of water in it. This supplied enough for the cattle housed in the barn, but not enough for the house. As winter closed in there was no sign of a break in the weather. Between the middle of October and the end of December it rained on only three days. We had our first sight of what became a familiar spectacle – the strange appearance of a frozen countryside with no ice and no frost as the atmosphere had become so dry it could not yield up even a few crystals of frozen water.

We grappled with this first shortage with a few straightforward measures. We took no baths, but relied on a wash and sponge down. I washed our clothes at the launderette in the nearby town. We drew on our only reserves of water – the second well and the dew-pond. By the beginning of November the taps were almost permanently dry and we started to rely on water from our second well. Bucketful after bucketful had to be pumped by hand and tipped into tanks on a trailer behind a tractor. About eighty gallons a day – forty buckets of water at ten swings on the pump per bucket.

As the autumn continued we grew increasingly aware of the subtle changes in the life of the countryside around us that presaged a change in the weather. Some are well enshrined in British folklore: cattle lying down during the day, just as a red sky in the morning means mackintoshes and Wellingtons. Some were peculiar to our farm. On the rare occasions when rain was on the way we could see clearly the summit of Clee Hill in Shropshire on our northern horizon; we could hear the clatter of trains on the Shrewsbury to Cardiff line and the rumble of traffic on the trunk road to the west of us.

In the third week of December the smaller well also ran dry and we resorted to drawing water from the dew-pond, also by the bucketful. But relief was at hand. After only one day of our floundering about in the thick mud round the edge of the pond the rain came. Only a couple of days of showers fell at first to tide us over Christmas. Then in the New Year the skies opened and the monsoons finally arrived. They never seemed to stop for the next ten weeks. By March 1974 both wells were full to the brim and our first experience of drought was over. The wells continued to supply plenty of water for the next eighteen months. We put the hard period of that autumn out of our minds, as an aberration from the natural pattern of abundant rainfall which brought abundant well water. Our confidence was increased when we found in the spring that there had been an extra drain on our resources. Our farm had, until we bought it, been part of a bigger farm. Two troughs in our neighbour's field had been left connected to our system, and were being supplied from our tank.

When we bunged up the connecting pipe with a wooden stopper we found our supply went even further.

But our experience that autumn had worried us, and we discussed the idea of going on the mains. This was not because we did not care for our own well water. Generations of farmers had raised young families on it; many of them were still living in the area, and looked remarkably healthy. As the months went by it was clear the water had a high lime content which benefited both ourselves and the livestock. Horses with light, shelly feet which tended to crack and break grew strong, healthy hooves. Our own hair and fingernails also showed an improvement that no amount of pharmaceutical preparations could ever achieve.

In contrast the state of the mains water in Herefordshire was a perennial complaint that found its way regularly into the columns of the local newspapers. In our area neighbours complained that what came out of the taps resembled lemon barley water. So high was the lime content that tanks and pipes became blocked with fur only a few years after being installed. In the south of the county it was even worse. There, the water was often brown, particularly after storms had stirred up the rivers from which it was drawn. And in dry weather some mains supplies had proved to be polluted.

Nevertheless we decided we should get connected to the mains, as a precaution against future droughts. Then in the summer of 1974 the livestock market collapsed. As far as cattle were concerned Britain was neither in the Common Market nor out of it. The old market support system had been withdrawn and nothing had replaced it. Two warring parties at Westminster, with their eyes on the urban vote, let the countryside go hang. Our cattle sold for less than half the price they had made the previous year. We were left with a large loss to recoup, and with no reserves for the following year. All our major investment plans were shelved indefinitely. We sold any farm machinery and equipment we could spare and began a long struggle back to profitability. At least we were spared, in this period of nightmarish economic worry, any further worries about water. The summer of 1974 was wet and cold, and though the harvest was delayed, and haymaking was difficult, we knew that the underground water reserves must be by then well stocked.

We did not even really worry when the summer of 1975 proved

to be the hottest of the century. We were glad to luxuriate in the warmth. It was a marvellous year for haymaking, marvellous for straw-baling, and good for show jumping, for the ground remained reasonably soft. We moved into another autumn and winter in as optimistic a mood as any farmers dare allow themselves.

2. October 1975

When the blow fell on 15 October, and we suddenly realized that the main well was not replenishing itself but had fallen to the level of 1973, we still felt no deep worries. We thought the water shortage would be only temporary. After all, we said, this had happened before, two years back. Rainfall in September had been about average and we were pretty confident that the winter rains could come soon and replenish our supplies. All it meant was a few weeks of inconvenience in which we might have to cart water, limit our baths, and ration household usage.

We were, though, oddly shamed by our predicament and went to great lengths to keep it secret. This was partly because we thought it could become a great joke in the neighbourhood. Country people are generous and selfless when natural disasters strike. If you have an accident, for instance, or your barns burn down, they will work night and day to help you. But farming misfortunes are another story. Farmers revel in tales of their neighbour's mishaps as if to ward off ill luck to themselves. To an outsider this might seem callous light-heartedness, but to each other it is a robust reaction to their daily battle with the elements.

'Have you seen Sanderson's hay crop?' they say gleefully. 'It's as black as tar. Won't be fit for nothing 'cept a match. Never could make hay.'

As the theme warms up the narrator begins to heave with laughter. 'Year after year. Always cuts his hay then woosh, down comes the rain.'

A fall in cattle prices is guaranteed to cause some merriment to those who do not need to sell at that time.

'Did you hear what Davis's cattle made in the market? Only

£25 a hundredweight. And he's been pushing the grub at them, really pushing the grub at them, all winter.' More laughter. 'He's done all that work and it's cost him money.'

But our reluctance to make our problem public may also have had deeper roots. For hundreds of years the water supply has been the most crucial factor in livestock farming. Through the ages farms and, on occasions, whole villages like Tetsworth in Oxfordshire, have been forced to move when the water table shifted. We had just a vague, undefined fear that our farm might become a dead loss for stock, winning a bad name which would be tied to it for years.

We were not alone in being reticent. As the winter of 1975–76 progressed the drought became more severe and many hundreds of families were affected. Stories of water shortages began to circulate, but the victims were seldom named. This was an odd fact in a society where gossip is the main form of communication and slander is bandied about with gay abandon.

More obviously, our business in horses would have taken a knock if it became public knowledge that we were out of water. At times, though, there was little we could do to conceal it. In the middle of October a client arrived with a horse to be schooled before the start of the hunting season. We settled it in a loose box with a tidy bed of fresh straw. To provide it with water, I put the stable bucket under the tap of the rainwater tank outside. To my horror the tap just dribbled pitifully as the last few drops drained from the tank. There was a little water in some of the other tanks stationed at strategic points round the farm. To this day I do not know what that client thought as she watched me upended as I leant right into one tank after another, legs kicking in the air to keep my balance, until I had filled the bucket. But she left her horse with us.

In the middle of October Tom's sister and brother-in-law came to stay with us for the weekend. They had not seen us for two years, since just after we moved to the farm. In those days you needed fishing waders to make it to the back door through the three feet of thick slurry in the farmyard. The stone buildings were faced with bits of corrugated tin and rotting timber while any holes were patched with what turned out to be flattened sardine tins. The house had its own charms: rising and falling damp, peeling paintwork and a mortar on parts of the outside walls which bore a peculiar resemblance to dried Herefordshire mud.

My sister-in-law, an estate agent with experience of the trauma of doing-up old properties, had predicted that it would take us five years to get the place straight. But in two years we had filled the yard with stone, rebuilt the derelict buildings into neat rows of loose boxes and made the house fairly habitable. We were enormously proud of the transformation we had made, and they were most impressed with our work. Yet we were reluctant to admit that our small holding still lacked the most basic and essential amenity of all – running water.

In particular we were concerned that the normal flushing of the lavatory by our visitors would be a big drain on our meagre resources. To preserve our secret we crept out at midnight and armed with torches we crouched over the well trying to knock the pump into life to draw up what little water had collected in the previous twelve hours.

On the whole, though, the visit from Tom's sister and brother-in-law was a welcome break for us in an autumn dominated by worry about water. Most of the stock was still out at grass and drank from the dew-pond, so life on the farm itself had not been greatly disrupted by the water shortage. Tom's brother-in-law, James, is a huge and normally taciturn man. But that weekend he proved to be a true English yeoman at heart. He threw himself into the work with gusto, marching across the pasture in his size-twelve Wellington boots singing noisily, 'To be a farmer's boy'.

He was less impressed with the vegetable garden. He laughed outright at my sparse collection of cabbages stranded in a patch of bare earth and threatened on all sides by a decaying jungle of weeds and remarked: 'It looks as though you spend all of half an hour a week in there.' Tom and I exchanged glances. Little did he know the hours we spent in that enclosed plot, not tending the vegetables but peering helplessly down the dark and almost dry well.

They never did discover the truth about our water problems that winter. We told them the full story the following summer but by that time there was nothing unusual about our predicament.

By the beginning of November the well was down to about ten gallons a day – just over five buckets. We were by now seasoned campaigners in the battle to save water. We set in train again the techniques we had employed two years earlier, in the 'little drought' of 1973, and steadily discovered new ones. By the year's end we were familiar with all the little tricks to save water that many of Britain's households were to be forced to adopt by the late summer of 1976. In fact, we soon became quite manic about saving water; every time a visitor to the farm turned on a tap we twitched with apprehension.

Luckily for us water from the taps had perforce always been used sparingly in our household. This is more by accident than by design. At the best of times the pressure in the taps is low. When the bath is being run no water comes through into the kitchen. There was never any chance that anyone would waste two gallons cleaning their teeth; it takes at least five minutes to get a bucketful out of our system.

But our archaic plumbing system had one major drawback during the drought. The pipes take such a circuitous route through the ground floor of the house that about a gallon of cold water has to be run off the hot tap before any hot water appears. This was water we could not afford to waste. When washing-up or bathing the baby I caught this cold water in a preserving pan and heated it up on the stove to use later. But it was a time-consuming business so Tom and I gradually hardened ourselves to washing in cold water.

That autumn we learnt quickly the main lesson about saving water within the house, the lesson which was in a few months' time to be featured in a multitude of newspaper articles as the drought reached the home hints pages of the newspapers. This is that the biggest economy is to flush the lavatory only when absolutely necessary. The simple action of emptying the cistern, such an integral part of our civilization, probably accounts for about a third of the water used by the average household. We had to drill ourselves not to flush it automatically, but to do so only when necessity demanded it. Indeed we gradually slipped into the habit of flushing it only two or three times a day, so that when we visited friends who faced no such problems we had to make a conscious effort to revert to former habits.

When there was no water in the pipes leading to the cistern, we kept a bucket nearby, took the lid off the cistern – luckily it was a low one – and filled it from the bucket. In this way we recycled washing water, or rainwater from a special tank outside when the water was unfit for the animals to drink. At first we used old washing-up water, but this proved too dirty. It formed a greasy slime inside the cistern, developed an unpleasant smell, and bits of malodorous debris collected in the bottom.

About that time I had to take one of the horses we had at livery for a day's cub-hunting and my neighbour, Jan Bolt, came to babysit with her two-year-old daughter, Sally. When they had gone we discovered to our surprise that we were out of water even though we had put the pump on that morning. Then the explanation dawned: Sally, who was just toilet trained, must have gone to the lavatory four or five times and, with a couple of visits by her mother, they had conscientiously flushed away our entire supply of water for the next two days.

The main headache was finding enough water for the baby. He had been born that summer, and fortunately I was breast-feeding him. This cut out the need for gallons and gallons of water to wash and sterilize bottles. Nappies were the main problem. For a time I battled on with the towelling ones, trudging round the farm to the rainwater tanks to rinse them. And when the rainwater was used up I drove the car over the firm dry fields to do them at the hand pump in the bottom field. When that failed I reckoned the housekeeping budget would have to bear the cost of disposable paper nappies. But the paper ones never managed to cope with the half-pint of orange juice that the baby insisted on downing just before he went to bed. So I was still left with quite a pile of towelling nappies to take to the launderette with the rest of the household washing. The local launderette was beginning to be well-patronized by the growing number of farming and village victims of the drought. Living on a farm means clean clothes are essential. A pair of jeans may last a city dweller for a week before they need washing. But there are few things more unpleasant or damaging to one's morale than to walk around smelling like a cow shed. The clothes-washing just had to be done.

After a long day on the farm, the twice-weekly trips to the launderette became a real chore. However carefully I timed my visits, the launderette always seemed to have half the machines out of action and the other half monopolized by the local hair-dresser putting through 150 towels, or by a soccer club supporter washing the jerseys and socks of the entire first, second and third elevens. The British queueing system was completely unknown and any attempt to introduce it was met with loud abuse.

Whenever there was any rainwater I therefore struggled to do the washing at home by hand. By using the spinning programme on my automatic machine between washing and rinsing it was possible to do a load of dirty clothes in four gallons of water. At first it seemed out of the question to use the washing machine itself because it had to be connected to the taps. But after considering the mechanics we did work out a way it could be filled manually and then used on the rinse programme.

Our clothes were usually clean but our standards of personal hygiene inevitably slipped as the winter months passed. The baby had top priority with the clean water. He had a daily bath in a small basin with about a gallon and a half of water. At first we re-used the water for washing ourselves – standing in the bath, soaping all over and then having a quick sluice-off. But as the weather grew colder the water cooled too rapidly for us and even a brisk rub with a bath towel in front of the living-room fire did little to restore the circulation. In the end we made do with a more cursory wash and an occasional bath when it rained or when we visited friends.

In the kitchen the saving of water took careful organization. The same water was used for washing all the vegetables, by starting with the greens and ending with the dirtier ones like potatoes. Cooking itself need not take much water. For gastronomic reasons I have always cooked vegetables in as little water as possible. Greens like cabbage I cooked over a pan of something like potatoes.

After a few weeks I became highly skilled too at washing-up in half a bowl of water. I managed to deal with the after-effects of a meal for four in just two gallons of water.

City friends who came to see us that winter regarded our relatively waterless way of life with amusement. It reinforced the distorted impression of rural life they had gained from newspapers and television and from their occasional forays into the countryside on sunny summer days. The environmentalists with their doom-laden predictions of the effects of agro-industry may have killed off the image of the smock-garbed yokel chewing a straw. But the concept of the sturdy but crude countryman persists. The breakfast-food and pipe-tobacco advertisements, together with kitchen-sink-type dramas set among the pig troughs, have projected a picture of life on small British farms which is only marginally less outdated.

A friend from Birmingham summed up the feelings of many of our visitors. We were standing in the farmyard on a bright cold winter afternoon describing our water problems when she said: 'Heavens. Living in a town we never think about water. I mean you turn on the tap and out it comes. It always has and I suppose it always will do.' She glanced about her with a fresh wariness and caught sight of several uneven tiles on the roof. 'Is your roof falling off too?' she asked.

'Intermittently,' we replied.

She shivered apprehensively and huddled into her thick knitted jacket. 'What you people in the country have to put up with. Do you have proper drains or anything like that here?'

Our rural neighbours, on the other hand, were full of practical advice when they became aware of our predicament. Many of them were battling with the same problem. I discovered to my surprise how even in 1975 piped mains water was regarded as something of a luxury in the country areas of Herefordshire.

Though Herefordshire is renowned for its water, the mains supplies are limited outside the towns. Villages and hamlets are served by scattered service reservoirs, rivers and bore-holes – and there are many gaps. When the drought became news, one local television news programme reported that 60000 people in Herefordshire depended on private supplies. These homes are usually easy to identify: they have a spaghetti-junction arrangement of storm-water pipes from the roof guttering that channels the rainwater into a tank by the back door.

Several of the cottages in our own village, mainly the homes of old-age pensioners, have only tanks like that and an outside well for water. In an attempt to do something in this difficult situation, the local Social Services Department collects the old people and takes them into town once a week for a bath. Life in country villages is a good deal more complicated than the passing motorist would think.

Securing a supply of mains water in Herefordshire could be a long job. In 1976, for instance, in the two neighbouring areas of Orleton Common and the Goggin, the residents had been waiting for water for eighteen years. A scheme was first drawn up in 1958 and at one time pipes were even loaded on a lorry in readiness for work to start. But they were needed elsewhere and the scheme never did get underway. It was an extreme case but delays of several years were common. Local people remarked wryly that the Water Board must have a special load of nomadic pipes which toured the county and which, from time to time, could be dumped temporarily in areas where residents were becoming restless over the long delays.

The lack of mains water meant that many farmers' wives of my own generation had coped with young families in conditions which would shock an urban social worker. Often the only supply of water for the house came from a hand pump over the sink or from a well outside the back door. When I asked how they had managed, their general response was a cheerful, 'what you've never had, you never miss'. After a few moments thought, several added, 'It was much worse for my mother. She didn't have a twin-tub washing machine.'

For it was the appearance of the twin-tub washing machine which transformed the lives of these women. Not only could it be used to wash and spin clothes, but it also served as a water heater. The machine could be filled with buckets, and heated like a conventional boiler. It was also a boiler, which had the enduring advantage of pumping water straight into the sink, so eliminating the messy and heavy job of filling and lifting buckets. I do not know who invented the twin-tub washing machine but he deserves to the full every penny he may have made from it.

3. November and December 1975

November: a month that evokes childhood memories of dark, drizzly evenings and damp Guy Fawkes nights. But November 1975 stayed dry, and we had reached the stage where we were resigned to the dry spell lasting until the New Year. Sunday's television weather forecast for farmers and growers became compulsory viewing in our isolated farmhouse. Week after week it showed the same map with the same prediction: no change.

In our pessimistic moods the idea crept up on us that there was a real possibility the drought could last all winter. And that posed the problem of watering the cattle when they were brought into the barns for the winter, from the end of December onwards. About a dozen of the smaller cattle were already housed in loose boxes. These were watered by hand, along with the horses, from the rainwater tanks. The rest of the stock was still out at grass and drank from the pond.

When the cooler weather came they were let into the sheds at night for a feed of barley, oat straw and some warmth. Normally when housed inside for the winter the animals drank from automatic water bowls. These are galvanized containers, the size of a soup bowl, with a tongue-shaped lever. When the animal drinks from the bowl it cannot avoid pressing the lever with its nose, whereupon the bowl refills automatically. As soon as the beast removes its head it releases the lever and the water stops. But now we tied the levers with string, so that however hard the cattle nuzzled them they could not depress them to release the water and so had to wait until they were let out in the morning for a drink. But the bowls did not always remain inoperative. Cattle will fiddle with anything, working away for hours with infinite patience – and the drinking bowls were an irresistible temptation. On several mornings we awoke to find all our precious water had been quaffed by the cattle during the night. One red and white Hereford yearling we called Rosie was an absolute expert at it. Many an evening I turned on the kitchen tap to find the pressure even lower than usual. I would rush out into the yard to see Rosie indulging in a long drink.

It began to get cold, and we knew that the cattle had to be housed in the barns permanently by the end of December at the latest. Without the automatic bowls working we had two choices. The first was to put troughs in the pens and fill them by hand; but that would involve carting considerable quantities of water and cleaning out the troughs almost daily as cattle are not particular about where they discharge their waste matter. The other alternative was to run the cattle out to the pasture to drink from the pond for an hour or two every day. This idea also had its snags. Without a readily available supply of water cattle tend to put on less weight. And being without water all night, they would gallop off into the field in the morning and run off still more weight.

In the middle of November the situation looked less bleak. One morning, with mounting excitement, we realized we could hear the trains on the Cardiff–Shrewsbury line a couple of miles away and the traffic on the main road – a sure sign that rain was on the way. There was nothing mysterious about that; it just indicated that the wind was coming from the west. The next day the first rain we had seen for over a month came down heavily and persistently. It dampened the spirits of the local hunt which was having its opening meet but sent ours soaring. I tackled a huge pile of dirty nappies, revelling in the luxury of having a plentiful supply of rainwater in the tank by the back door.

But this was to prove only a temporary reprieve. The following day was dry; not even a faint whisper of the trains could be detected. Treacherously, the wind had changed direction again, bringing more dry weather from the east. Soon after that the second well in the back field gave out. I had taken down a pile of the ubiquitous wet nappies, and had just finished washing them when the pump let out a gasping sigh followed by a sort of rusty death-rattle as it drew air instead of water.

It was an ominous portent. Over the next couple of days we

finished every drop of rainwater on the farm. We even emptied the dregs from an old sink which had been abandoned in the spinney and from the wheelbarrow left in the kitchen garden. Finally we loaded one of the empty rainwater tanks onto a trailer and Tom set off with it behind the tractor to our nearest neighbours, the Bolts, who live a mile away. For the first time we were having to seek water from outside our own boundaries.

Driving down in the car I was surprised to see we were not the only people carting water that frosty Sunday morning. We passed two other farmers on the same errand rumbling along the narrow country lane.

The Bolts were full of sympathy. Jan's father, it turned out, was already being forced to cart water for stock in a distant field normally served by a deep well. It had run dry for the first time anyone could remember. While George rushed around to find an old door, and some of the polythene he used to line his silage pit, to cover our tank, Jan stretched their Sunday lunch to go round all of us. They cheered us up considerably. We had good companions in our misfortune. Oh well, we thought, as we rolled home, this cannot go on for ever. As we watered the stock we sang part of the song we had composed two years before amidst the muck and filth around the farm.

> Oh what the hell
> There's no water in the well
> The cow ain't chewing the cud
> And the Triumph's stuck in the mud.

We had forgotten the rest of it.

By the time December arrived there had still been no proper rain and the well was bone-dry. Just to tantalize us there were a couple of heavy hailstorms. We watched with a feeling of sickening helplessness as the hailstones bounced off the roofs and onto the ground, well out of range of the tanks.

We had had some fresh hope when at first the nightly frosts yielded a few gallons of moisture for the rainwater tanks. But the frosts stopped as the air became drier and drier. We woke up morning after morning to a bare, stark countryside tinted by a hard, yellow light instead of the normal soft bluish-mauve of early winter. Clee Hill, marking the distant horizon, was forever capped in a gossamer haze – a sure sign there was no rain in the offing. In the evenings the sunsets were spectacular; the red, watery sun seemed to saturate the dusk. It prompted us to say:

> Red sky at night:
> Everyone's uptight.

Tom was now collecting a 200-gallon load of water almost daily from the Bolts. This we used for the stock housed inside. The water became a bit mucky after a few farmyard buckets had been dipped in it, so was unsuitable for the house except for flushing the lavatory and for washing floors. I collected our domestic supplies in two five-gallon containers.

We owe the Bolts a great deal for their kindness during this period. There was always a cup of tea for Tom while he waited for the tank to fill. Jan had to put up with me tramping through her living-room to fill my containers in the bathroom, sometimes under the startled gaze of her dinner-party guests or the ladies from the local Women's Institute.

The men at the local Meteorological Office were also helpful. We always rang them before setting off for water, in the hope our journey would not be necessary. On the couple of occasions it did rain, they saved us an unnecessary journey down the road.

As November went on the situation began to depress us thoroughly. The winter is a bad time on any farm. Much of the day, every day of the week, you do the same chores of feeding the stock. You grind corn, fill mangers, and carry endless bales of fodder and litter straw from the stackyard to the cattle sheds. You do this in the early morning dark and in the early evening dusk. At times we felt like automatons. When we had finished the morning chores and seen to the horses, the middle stretch of the day was filled with the water problem. It took Tom well over two hours to collect the water from the Bolts. Then we had to water by hand all the stock inside. We must have carried a hundred bucketfuls of water every day from the tank to the stock troughs.

Collecting water for the house also took about an hour. One can hardly dash through a neighbour's house into the bathroom, fill one's container and then disappear. Good manners – and one's natural desire for a gossip – decree that one must stop for a chat and a cup of tea if it is offered.

Both outside on the farm and in the house it was as though the clock had been turned back thirty years. With no water in the

B

taps there was, of course, no hot running water. Every drop for washing hands, dishes and the baby had to be heated in a preserving pan on the kitchen range. I soon realized that piped mains water is the most underrated convenience of the twentieth century. It must have contributed far more to the liberation of women than all the laws Parliament has put on the statute books in the past few years.

It is not only that carrying and heating water in the home makes extra work. It is above all time-consuming. We found it slowed down our rate of activity considerably. How often, for instance, do people turn on the taps to rinse their hands? Dozens of times in a normal day. We could not do this at all. We kept a basin of cold water in the sink, but we had to go to the Aga range for the hot water whenever we wanted to wash our hands properly, which was pretty often as we were working with animals. Even a trip to the lavatory meant a trudge outside first to collect a bucket of water. Indeed we were learning the most fundamental lesson of the drought – that shortage of water means a shortage of something even more precious – of time.

It was for the little jobs that I most missed running water. Washing out the milking bucket after extracting our daily four pintas from the house-cow was quite a task. So was rinsing the inside of the game birds on which we relied for many a winter meal. When the baby woke unexpectedly at night for a drink of fruit juice there was no hot water on tap to warm the bottle. It meant my going downstairs, filling a saucepan from the water container, using that to fill the kettle and then heating it.

We were not the only people scanning the sky for rain that month. Tom made several trips to market to sell our remaining lambs and learnt that the drought was not confined to our area. Markets are a major source of news for country people; they are as important as newspapers are to people living in towns. In a large market like Hereford buyers come from all over Britain. What happens in Scotland on one day is news in the Midlands the next. But at the market the drought in the immediate county was the big news. What was happening in Herefordshire itself was the main talking point. The drought, it appeared, was even worse in the south of the county. Some farmers had been without water since late summer. Now deep bore-holes were beginning to run dry. Elderly, retired farmers, whose gaunt, shrivelled figures haunt every market, were particularly pessimistic. They pronounced with due gravity that they could never remember anything like it. Wells that had provided water for generations had run out. People spoke apprehensively of what might hit them in the coming months.

Not only were the wells and ponds going dry; at the end of the first week of December came a clear indication that the mains water supplies were in trouble. The Medical Officer of Health at Ross-on-Wye pronounced that the water drawn from a place called Castlebrook was still not fit to drink. Castlebrook was an important feeder of reservoirs, yet the Castlebrook complex was itself an old problem of the water system. It served an upland area, including Howle Hill, the highest point in the county, which was about five miles south of Ross and just inside the border with Gloucestershire. Two service reservoirs, one half-way up Howle Hill and the other near the top, had water pumped into them from Castlebrook. The original bore-hole near the brook had proved insufficient for the growing needs of the area and twelve years before a temporary pump had been installed to extract water directly from the brook. The pump was still there, nestling under its temporary tarpaulin cover. Constant trouble with the filtering equipment meant that water in the taps in the area was often brown and sometimes polluted.

Back in the summer of 1975 the water had been found to be highly contaminated – perhaps not too surprising considering the high temperatures and low rainfall. Now as mid-winter approached the results of tests were still not acceptable. Samples taken at several points showed that over 5 per cent contained *coeliform bacilli* or *E celli* disease-carrying bacteria. In other words it meant that the water did not come up to government standards.

This was only the start of the water troubles for the people living near Howle Hill. Two days later the reservoirs dried up completely. The Water Authority laid on four tankers carrying up to 5000 gallons each in a round-the-clock operation to ferry water from Gloucestershire to the middle reservoir. This eased the situation, but many homes and farms in the upland areas remained without water. An assortment of tankers from the army, milk transporters, and even the fire brigade, were used to take water to central areas for householders to collect their own supplies in buckets.

It soon became clear that the farmers in the Howle Hill area, particularly those with dairy herds, were as hard-hit as we were, even though they were on the mains. Because of engineering difficulties people served by the middle reservoir had priority. When the level there dropped no water reached the top reservoir and the homes and farms served from it went without. No one knew from one day to the next whether there would be any water in the taps. Farmers began to rage against the Water Authority, which did not monitor the reservoirs continuously. It was left to the householders to phone up when the supply failed. Farmers complained bitterly that it took at least a day for the authority to get its colourful convoy of hired tankers rolling.

When the water did arrive it was often not enough. Initially only small tankers carrying 200 or 300 gallons were used. Some dairy farmers with sixty to seventy cows were having to manage on 200 gallons a day when they needed six times that amount. After a few weeks larger tankers were pressed into service. But that presented the problem of where to store the daily delivery of water. Farms on the mains do not usually have spare 2000-gallon tanks lying around.

They had a determined spokesman in Gerry Evans, chairman of the Ross-on-Wye branch of the National Farmers' Union. 'We need it regularly and we get it intermittently,' he said. 'It is not only harmful for the animals to be starved of water, it is also dangerous. You can't get them to queue up like you can with human beings.' We took note, for our own use if need be, of the advice Mr Evans gave a distraught farmer. He suggested he should ring the RSPCA. 'It seemed to me to be the only thing to do.'

We followed these troubles, as they unfolded day by day in the papers, with close attention. It was some consolation for us to think that even if we had gone onto the mains, all our troubles might not have ended. We were also getting to know, through the reports of this dispute, a body which was going to play an increasingly important part in our lives – the Welsh National Water Development Authority. The shortage at Howle Hill was the first real test of their ability to deal with a drought. It seemed to us that their basic policy did not greatly differ from the one we had had to adopt on our farm – to gamble on the rains coming, and in the meanwhile to get by as best one could. It was some time before they announced any major step to improve the supply. Finally the authority said that it planned to install a two-and-a-half-mile overland pipe from the River Wye, but they still warned people that there was no guarantee that they would have water back in their pipes by Christmas.

These troubles at Ross had serious implications for the rest of the county. The Water Authority warned that it was tapping supplies elsewhere to help Ross. Contingency plans for rationing had been drawn up. It was the first time that such a drastic word as 'rationing' had come into the discussion. We also had the first of those pleas for self-rationing which were to echo throughout the coming months. Compulsory rationing, said the Water Authority, could be avoided if people throughout the county practised strict economies.

On our own farm we needed no such adjuration. A real crisis-point was reached in the middle of December. Tom went down with a feverish cold, yet he could not stay in bed because he still had to cart water daily for the stock. We tried to reduce the burden by carting a double load, but the effort came so near to disaster that we decided not to risk it again. The tyres on the tractor spun wildly on the icy lane's surface as it strained to haul the extra weight up the hill. If we had not eventually made it up the lane we would have been forced to empty one of the tanks, baling it out with buckets. Since high banks lined the lane on both sides the only place to chuck the water would have been on the road itself. Here it would have frozen solid, forming in effect a narrow glacier which would have isolated us and the two cottages nearby.

After some hard thought we decided we would have to dip into our slender cash reserves and get a tanker-load of water delivered. The water could be pumped into the cisterns in the barn and we would then have water in the taps in the house and in the drinking bowls in the cattle sheds. However expensive it might be, it would give us a much-needed breather over Christmas. So we set about discovering how one purchased water for delivery.

We found that until two years ago the fire brigade had done the job, delivering water in their tankers. But since the Water Resources Act of 1973, the job had been taken over by the newly established water authorities.

I rang the local office of the Water Authority. It gave me

my first chastening taste of involving bureaucracy in one's affairs.

'Yes, we do deliver water,' said the official, 'but not this month. The tanker is on loan to the Ministry of Agriculture at Worcester for three weeks. Try again after Christmas.

'No, I'm sorry, there's no one else who delivers water. It's our job. You'll have to wait till the New Year.'

I decided to invoke the aid of the welfare state. I called at the Social Services Department of the local council. I explained my husband was ill, I had a five-month old baby and no water.

'Ring this number,' said the girl. 'It's the Water Authority.' I explained the problem. 'Then ring the County Council.'

The County Council was equally helpless. 'Try the fire brigade' they suggested. 'Oh no, they don't do it anymore. I'll give you the number of the Water Authority. Oh well, if they can't help, no one can. There's nothing we can do.'

As a last resort I tried the local office of the Ministry of Agriculture. The man I spoke to was sympathetic. He was stumped by the problem but promised to look through some back numbers of the National Farmers' Union journal to see if any private firm advertised a water-carrying service. He failed to come up with anything, but at least he had tried. There was really nothing for it but for my husband to muffle himself up and, cold or no cold, take the tractor and the tank back down the lane.

Somehow, without any help from a tanker-load, we survived this bad period. We were even able to muster a sympathetic laugh when a client who farms several hundred acres in Gloucestershire came to see us. His problems were acute – but the reverse of ours.

'I would be quite happy to spend the rest of my days in a place like this,' he said. 'You may have no water, but then every place has its problems. My farm is flooded out almost every spring. At least there's no chance of that happening here.'

As the months wore on the shortage hit one neighbour after another. In the middle of December we heard that two more cottages near the village had run out of water. Ted Rivers, who runs a thirty-five-acre small holding five miles away, was another victim. Every day he collected twenty-five milk churns of water for his stock and his farmhouse.

He did this even though he had bought a trailer-tanker in the autumn in case the situation became desperate. In the interval he had lent it to Stan Phillips, another neighbour, who rented some additional grazing without a water supply about seven miles away. Borrower and lender drifted into deadlock as to who should collect the tanker from this distant field. Each argued that it was the other's agreed responsibility.

This altercation developed into a minor feud over the next few months, watched with the fascination which such a battle of wills arouses in a small community. These were both men of the Marches, instinctively determined to hold their ground. Eventually in the spring, honour was satisfied. Phillips returned the tanker, and the incident faded, not into insignificance, but into the folklore of the village.

Then Christmas week brought us the best of all seasonal gifts. Two days before Christmas it rained for the first time in six weeks. All the rainwater tanks filled up, so we were spared the task of carting water over Christmas. If we could not call it a holiday, we could at least turn it into a feast day. We heated up water on the stove in the preserving pan and saucepans for the ultimate luxury – a bath in our own bathroom. Mountains of washing were done, stables were sluiced out and disinfected and the car, for so long camouflaged by dirt, was washed.

4. January 1976

The first weekend of the New Year saw the first real rain for months. And it came with a vengeance. At midday on Friday an eerie stillness descended on the countryside. For half the winter we had lived in a muffled world with no clank of distant trains, no rumble of vehicles on the trunk road and no sounds of water – no melting frost dripped off buildings, no splash of tyres, no surface water trickling through the turf and no squelch of our Wellies as we walked across the pasture. Now there was total silence; no birds singing, no trees creaking and no hedgerows rustling in the breeze.

Over to the west a false dawn spread over the Welsh hills, slowly turning the whole sky a menacing, bloodshot pink. High above us tufts of dark cloud scudded across the sky – a particularly spooky sight as there was no wind at ground level.

We, of course, were totally unprepared for a storm. The wind began to rise in a low apprehensive whisper just as Tom was completing the installation of a lighting circuit in one of the lines of loose boxes. Somehow he had managed to arrange the system so that half the lights were illuminated when the switch was on and the other half when it was off. After various desperate attempts to rectify the situation it was obvious that to switch all the lights off at once we would either have to keep removing half the bulbs or summon professional assistance.

I was dispatched to town to collect the electrician. As I started the car the first drops of rain struck the windscreen. Five minutes later rain was teeming down, bouncing off the roofs of the old stone cottages that huddled round the pub. In the garden of the retired postman's cottage the autumn flowers that had bloomed on into the winter had been smashed to confetti.

The town looked as though it was in the middle of an air raid. Hardly a soul moved in the streets. People jammed the pavements under the overhanging buildings and every now and then some brave individual would hoist his coat onto his head and make a heroic dash for the next sheltered spot on his route.

I spotted the electrician, standing quite unconcerned under the greengrocer's awning. Coatless and hatless, he strolled over to the car. He told me his parents had been without water for two months. The storm would at least replenish their rainwater tanks. Back at the farm he diagnosed the trouble in about two minutes flat. The switch was at the wrong end of the circuit, which itself was wired up back to front.

Throughout the evening the storm built up to hurricane proportions. The wind roared and screamed through the dense screen of oaks that bordered the western side of the farm. The house seemed to shake on its foundations and from time to time there was a tearing crack followed by an ominous thud as a branch was wrenched from a tree. We went to bed feeling the end of the world was coming.

But by the morning the storm had vanished. It was one of those incredibly clear, warm winter days when the sun shines strongly from an intensely blue sky. If someone had put the leaves back on the trees it could have been summer. The damage was clear enough too. A dozen slates embedded in the lawn like tombstones indicated there was a new skylight in the roof. More slates were missing from the buildings, two sheets of corrugated iron had been ripped off the back of the barn and the telephone was dead.

The silent telephone was no surprise. Back in the autumn a contractor on our neighbour's land had sliced through the cable with a mechanical digger. By the time the Post Office arrived to replace it the corn was planted and the cable had to be left hitched up on the hedge instead of running underground. Whenever the hedge was disturbed by the local hunt, by poachers or by stray animals, the cable fell off, dislocating the delicate connection to the telegraph pole and leaving us without communication with the wider world.

We walked over the fields in the crisp sunshine and found to our relief that the actual damage was slight, though the storm had left us enough firewood to last for the next five years. It looked as though a giant with a huge hatchet had gone berserk in the night. The top of one of the five pines planted to mark the ancient ridgeway that is now our bumpy drive had been snapped clean off. Two hawthorn trees had been torn up by the roots, an elderly oak had split down the middle. And everywhere there was fallen wood: great branches, sticks and twigs carpeted a good ten acres of land along the woodside.

Thankful for once for the good weather, we turned our backs on the mess, collected ladders and ropes and set about the job of repairing the roof. We were old hands at it; when we first moved to the farm we spent at least one day a week up the ladders. After every session Tom would remark confidently: 'There, that ought to hold it.' A few days later there would be more slates on the lawn.

This time the roof had done us proud. As Tom put it: 'What's twelve slates in a hurricane?' Some of our neighbours had not got off so lightly. As we drove down to the Bolts' that afternoon we saw fruit trees uprooted, barns with gaping sides, smashed greenhouses, and chimneys reduced to a pile of rubble on the ground.

The next day the rain was back. As it thundered down on our newly repaired roof we thought the long awaited monsoons had arrived. The weather appeared to be staging a repeat performance of its behaviour two years before. The pattern was exactly the same – to the very day. First a few showers to tide us over Christmas and then a severe storm heralding the arrival of a long wet spell.

But it was not to be. This time it heralded a long dry spell. What the weathermen called 'those persistent areas of high pressure' moved smartly back into position and rapidly dried out the whole of southern Britain once again.

Up till then our arrangements for coping with the water shortage had only been makeshift. We had assumed the problem would be temporary. But the perversely dry weather that now set in convinced us that the rainless spell could last through the rest of the winter and into the spring and summer. So we began to make plans to manage more permanently if our own water supply stayed dry.

We scrutinized our bank statement and realized once again that a mains water supply was hopelessly expensive. But we did invest in a portable pump that could be powered by the tractor. This would enable us to draw water from the dew-pond. Every time we buy a new machine for the farm we wish we had done so months earlier, and so saved ourselves hours of time and trouble. The pump was no exception. It reduced the time we spent carting water to one hour a day.

As the dry days followed one upon another, the problems spread like a blight across the district. The vet came to castrate the bull calves. We managed to scrape together a bucket of water for him to wash his hands, and listened to his account of how the drought was affecting the whole area. Farm after farm that he visited was up against the same shortage of water. It was hitting with particular force those old-age pensioners whose pets formed an essential part of any country vet's practice. One old man was dependent upon a supply half a mile away. He walked that distance every day to collect all that he could carry – one bucketful.

Our worst problem continued to be that of watering the cattle. As soon as the bullocks could safely be penned with the heifers we sorted them into two bunches according to size and housed them in pens permanently for the rest of the winter. Since it was very difficult to get water to them, we decided to get them to the water. We let each group out into the dew-pond field for an hour each day. It meant considerable extra work. In a normal winter we needed only an hour to feed and fodder the lot. Now it took all morning. Each bunch in turn had to be chased out and herded back in again. To make matters worse the animals were bedded on deep litter. This meant that every day about two feet of compacted manure had to be dug away to enable us to open the gates of the pens – gates which would otherwise have stayed closed all winter.

Inside the house the situation eased slightly in mid-January as water from the New Year storm worked its way into the well. The level crept up a bare three inches, but that was enough to let us turn on the immersion heater and get water back into both the hot and cold taps. It was a great relief to have water back in the house. After my ill-fated attempts to secure a delivery by tanker I had one more go at the welfare establishment. When the baby went to the clinic for his injections I diffidently told the doctor I was finding it a struggle to manage without water. The doctor's reaction made me feel a complete fool.

'Well,' she said with breezy cheerfulness, 'I must say he looks marvellous. He's obviously doing very well on rainwater.'

But we moved into a period when he and I were not doing quite so well. Both of us began to suffer from infected scratches and spots. Any abrasion of the skin was likely to turn septic. The cause came to light when the rainwater tank outside the back door became empty: there was a large dead rat in the bottom.

We were, though, beginning to learn to live with the drought. It no longer seemed such a terrible hardship to be without constant hot and cold water. This had assumed the dimensions of merely a minor inconvenience. Yet there was a strangeness about life, as though we were living in a different world. It was not only that the countryside had altered subtly. It was the little things: cars arriving at the farm no longer swished through the puddles in the potholes on the drive. They arrived soundlessly on the farmyard before we had a chance to shut up our fierce alsatian who attacked all strangers – friend or foe – quite indiscriminately.

On the television the popular soap operas began to seem slightly foreign. One evening we were watching 'Crossroads'. Something about it seemed odd, as if the continuity department had slipped up somewhere. The characters were discarding wet mackintoshes and muttering about the terrible weather. That can't be the Midlands, I thought fleetingly, it never rains like that nowadays.

The electricity bill arrived and turned out to be £10 less than the previous year despite the enormous increase in charges. It was a reminder of how much less hot water we had been using.

All around us more and more people were being affected by the drought. On many mornings we passed an oldish man in a vast cap pumping water from the village brook into a 500-gallon tank. Up till then the only victims of the drought we knew of were villagers and small holders who relied for their water on ancient private supplies. But this man was no shoe-string farmer. From his powerful tractor, his modern trailer and his sophisticated diesel pump we assumed he came from a substantial and prosperous holding. 'The big boys are being affected now,' we remarked as we drove past. It was the first sign we had seen that deep bore-holes and major private resources were running low. In the village itself a mechanical digger was pulling up the road so that mains connections could be laid to cottages where wells had run dry.

Fears of a prolonged drought deepened when the Water Authority warned that in the south of the county there was still a 35 per cent shortfall in supplies and little prospect of any improvement until the following winter. At Ross the authority had got as far as surveying the route for its emergency pipeline. The necessary equipment had been ordered and work on the scheme was to start as soon as possible. But there was a hold-up while negotiations went on with local farmers for the right to cross their land. One of those nomadic loads of pipes had arrived at the bottom of a place called Bull's Hill to mark the progress of the scheme.

For those with water came the news that they would be paying more for it. After a 44 per cent increase the previous year charges to householders were going up another 17½ per cent, while for metered users the bill would be 12 per cent more.

Towards the end of January the weather changed at last. Just when the well went completely dry again snow began to fall. Overnight the fields and hedgerows were smothered in a thick foamy whiteness. Normally we loathed the snow. It was a formidable adversary.

In previous years when we had run sheep on the farm and wintered cattle outside we spent many long cold hours struggling across the pasture with bales of hay on our backs. During lambing we tried to herd inside the ewes on the point of parturition. The phrase 'silly sheep' is based on acute observation. All too often they would trot happily in front of us until they reached the farmyard gate. Then with a quick jump and an incredible turn of speed they would race back to the other side of the field followed by the sound of loud curses and the muffled crunch of Wellington boots in cold pursuit.

A snowfall of more than a few inches isolated us from the outside world. The farm road disappeared into a white wilderness. With no fences, banks or hedges to mark its direction as it bisected the fields, it was all too easy to lose track of it and drive straight onto the pasture and get firmly stuck. At the Micklebury Motorway end by the village conditions were even worse. We could see the direction of the road clearly enough: it ran down a cut between two twenty-foot banks. But on top of the road the snow collected in six-foot drifts.

But now the snow was welcome. Its arrival made us feel as if we were coming home from that strange dry land where we had been exiled for the past seven months. The barren arid countryside gave way to a soft grey and white world that was comfortingly familiar. On the other hand it turned the job of carting water into a nightmare.

On the second day I managed to get the car down the lane to go to the launderette. When I returned I found Tom had half-buried the tractor in the first mud of the winter by the pond. The second tractor turned out to have a flat battery and, because someone had driven it straight into the barn, it had to be reversed out. We managed to tow it out and then start it by using the stock lorry. Up at the dew-pond our problems started again. The wheels of the first tractor spun uselessly and worked deeper into the mud, while the second tractor reared up on its back tyres sending a shower of dry earth as it strained to pull the larger vehicle free. I had visions of our being forced to summon the building equipment contractors with their crane to get us out. But after a frightening two hours we managed to get both vehicles back onto dry land and made it safely back to the farm with our precious cargo.

I then set off through the snow again to Hereford to collect our new girl groom from the station. We had decided to take on some help as the show jumpers had to be prepared for the coming season. On our own we were only just managing to survive and somehow we had to make a living. We were a bit apprehensive that the girl would not stick the job once she discovered she was limited to one bath a week and had to take all her washing to the launderette.

But the drought was far more widespread than we had realized. Our new recruit, who was called Sarah, came from south Devon where, we learned, there was also a critical shortage of water. The stables where she had worked was lucky to be on the mains. It had been supplying water to several neighbouring farmers since the autumn. She accepted our shortages as a fact of life.

Sarah soon proved herself to be enthusiastic and hard-working. While life on our farm had its undeniable drawbacks they were slight compared with the conditions in her previous job. That had involved four hours of mucking out every day from seven until eleven o'clock every morning. She found our struggles in the house highly amusing and would double up with laughter as I prepared to wash up by heating rainwater on the kitchen range. Nor did she complain about conditions on the yard. Fetching water for the horses involved climbing up onto the trailer that held the tank of water pumped daily from the pond and it was no job for the clumsy-footed. Water from the tank got sloshed on the floor of the trailer and formed a skin of treacherous ice. One false step, which was easy enough to make when carrying two heavy buckets of water, and you skated straight off the end. But to Sarah it all seemed to be like a hilarious, badly organized camping holiday.

5. February and March 1976

The snow was short-lived. In the space of ten days it melted to a mucky slush and then disappeared into the thirsty ground. By the end of the first week of February the only evidence that there had been a break in the dry weather was a few inches of water in the rainwater tanks and a little more in the well. We were back in the land where the sun always shone and where white frosts and ice were unknown, however cold it was.

The weathermen were repeatedly predicting showers and rain in the outlook forecast. They never came. At the local meteorological office a duty officer explained: 'The rainfall peters out before it crosses the Welsh border. It's been so dry for so long the rain doesn't seem to be able to get into the country. Theoretically it should rain. But it doesn't.'

One evening as I was putting the baby to bed there was a sound like boots marching on the gravel in the farmyard. It was raining hard. As I went downstairs I could hear it trickling into the rainwater tank by the back door. Two hours later it stopped. It brought home to me the frightening change in the climate. 'What's happening?' I asked Tom. 'What's happening to the rotten weather? In a normal winter it would rain like that for a couple of days, then it would be dry and cold for a bit and then more rain. It's always dry now. Will things ever be normal again?'

More and more people were finding life increasingly abnormal. The Water Authority announced that it was to lay an emergency pipeline between Leominster and Hereford to provide water for people living between the two towns. According to one local councillor some people in the area had been reduced to catching rainwater for drinking.

In the south of the county the situation was even worse. Several whole villages were suffering from severe shortages. The worst case was a hamlet called Newtown. They had suffered, as a community, everything we had undergone as an isolated farm. Their problems now began to fill the local papers. Newtown is a scattered collection of a dozen houses and cottages in the beautiful countryside just four miles south of Hereford. The water supplies, always meagre, began to run out in September and dried up completely at the beginning of February. The villagers' only supply was a tiny well in the middle of a ploughed field half a mile away. The health authorities were worried that even that water was not fit to drink.

Families from the village had to visit relatives or the public baths in Hereford to keep clean, and washing was taken to the launderette in the city. Lavatories could not be flushed, central heating systems could not be used, fires remained unlit because of the risk to back boilers. Tap water was a long-forgotten luxury.

Even more galling was the fact that the village lay in the shadow of the giant reservoir at Aconbury. Newtown was also surrounded by a network of water mains, and the famous 'emergency' pipeline from the Wye was scheduled to pass within bucket-carrying distance. Two years before, the village had almost got a mains supply but the scheme was shelved. The Water Authority claimed the residents refused to sign the necessary contracts. But the villagers denied this. They still wanted the Water Authority to lay a pipeline to Newtown and to include in the scheme several other villages where private supplies were running low.

Faced with the prospect of months without water the villagers were up in arms and threatened to sit on the doorstep of 10 Downing Street. One old man had been collecting water from the well in the field for sixty-two years. He reckoned he walked 200 miles a year carrying water and remarked mildly he expected something better in 1976.

Most of the other householders had more modern arrangements until the drought struck. They had relied on nearby farms with deep bore-holes for their supplies. These had dried up one after the other over the previous five months. At least one farmer was faced with no alternative but to sell his stock. He had been managing with water delivered by tanker but it was proving prohibitively expensive. Nor was water by the tanker-load the answer to the ordinary householder's problems. One resident claimed the Water Authority had offered to deliver it by road, but at his own expense, which worked out at £25 for 200 gallons.

As far as a main supply was concerned the Water Authority maintained it would not be economic to run a pipeline to Newtown. The local district council was also unwilling to underwrite the scheme because it could see that other villages in the area would soon be out of water and Newtown could set an expensive precedent.

In other words no money could be found to provide a community with one of the essentials of life. Yet at that time the British Steel Corporation was reported to be losing £8 million a week and Chrysler had recently received a government handout of £130 million.

By the end of February it was glaringly obvious that the summer would see the greatest drought in Britain's history. Winter was almost over and rainfall had been minimal. The rivers around us – the Wye, the Severn, the Trent and the Teme – were at the lowest winter level ever recorded. There was the legacy of the previous long dry summer: rainfall in 1975 had been seven inches down on the previous year. On top of that, in the three winter water-gathering months till the end of January the rainfall had been barely two and a half inches, compared to almost seven inches in the same period in the previous year. Only continuous heavy rain in the next two months could avert what we feared would be a situation genuinely meriting the word 'catastrophe'.

We knew that after the end of April all the rain in the world could not save us. Summer rain has little effect on water resources. It all goes in evaporation or in transpiration by plants.

Now it was not only people like us with private supplies who were praying for rain. Throughout southern Britain water authorities were watching reservoir levels with grim forebodings. They had scraped through the drought the previous summer – but only just. At one point in August 1975, for instance, Derby had been only a week away from severe water rationing. Now television news showed us reservoirs in south Wales and in south-west England less than half full. The water authorities were blunt in their warning: barring torrential rain, amounting to at least twelve inches in the next two months, people in some areas would be rationed to five gallons a head a day by the summer.

A friend in Northamptonshire wrote to say the outlook in the east Midlands was bleak. Navigation on the canal that ran close to her home was being restricted because the locks could be opened only at critical times, to limit the amount of water used. Her letter expressed that disbelief, shared by so many throughout the rest of the year, that Britain could ever really have a drought. 'People are always predicting terrible natural disasters. Then they are averted at the last minute. After all, it's bound to rain.'

Even in death, it seemed, there was no escaping the water shortage. The local grave-digger, Ferdie, found the soil in the churchyard so hard that he had to water it before digging. In most places his job has been taken over by mechanical diggers, but in our area it is Ferdie, a garrulous septuagenarian complete with stutter and a magnificent stainless-steel spade, who digs the graves. He usually has a few choice words to offer on any subject. Now he remarked, with bemused candour: 'I've had to bail 'em plots out often enough, but I've never had to put water into 'em afore.' And when one of the families from our village attended a funeral in a hamlet five miles away, they noted that one bowl of water was all that was available to wash up the cups, plates and saucers after the funeral tea.

The melting snow had alleviated the shortage slightly, putting a few inches of water back into the well. We were now more concerned with the effect the freakish weather was beginning to have on our farmland and our livestock. The entire forty acres of our pasture were covered with an ugly acne of molehills. They erupted by the dozen overnight. At times it seemed there were more molehills than grass. Country lore held that these blind rodents pursued their open-scale mining activities during the wet winter because that was when their main quarry, the earthworms, came to the surface. During the summer the moles disappeared underground as the worms burrowed deeper to get to the wetter soils at lower levels. But in direct contradiction to this theory an army of moles was working overtime near the surface of our arid pasture. The same was true on many other farms in the area.

Our first thought was to call in the local mole catcher who charged 5p a mole. But an old farmer warned Tom. 'You dinna

wan to use him, boy, unless your pocket's real deep. Phillips had
'im in. 'Ee caught one hundred and thirty-five of the buggers on
ten acres. Oorh, din Phillips cough at the price.'

We rang the Ministry of Agriculture for advice. In due course
a man from the ministry arrived at the farm. He had a name like
Badger – I suspect it was Bageot – and the alert air of a hunter.
He was small, with tiny strong hands, and sharp black eyes. He
studied our lunar landscape with an expert gaze.

'Moles?' he queried briskly. 'Only one way to deal with them.
They have no natural predators. To get rid of them you've got to
kill them. Don't bother with those products they sell in town.
There are only three effective ways to deal with them.

'Mothballs. Good on small areas. Put them down in the runs
in your lawn and the moles will move off and pop up next door.
I did that last year. It worked well. My neighbour wasn't too
happy, though.

'Traps. Very effective for the odd one or two.

'Strychnine.' He rubbed his small hands. 'The only real way
when you've got a plague of them as you have out there. One
worm dipped in strychnine will kill ten moles – they eat their own
dead, you know.'

And off he went with Tom to show him where to put it. We
bought the poison, followed his instructions and three days later
there were no new eruptions in the night.

As the days lengthened and March arrived, borne in on icy winds
not like a lion but like a polar bear, we were faced with another
problem.

One cold morning of invisible frost I was feeding the stock
when I heard the unfamiliar sound of water dripping in the barn.
My first thought was that some idiot had left the hose-pipe on – a
capital offence on the farm punishable by a loud tirade of abuse.
The tap, though, was firmly off. One glance into the cattle shed
next to it solved the mystery. The roof was covered with a
stalactitic mass of icicles. Water was dripping down from them
so fast that the old manure on the floor beneath had risen six
inches with the water it had absorbed. Immediately above the
roof was the loft in which were the cisterns that stored the water
pumped up from the well. It looked as if one of them had sprung
not just one leak but a whole sieveful.

When I climbed up into the loft my fears were confirmed.

Over the months when the cisterns had stood empty one of them had been attacked by rust. When the well had revived, and water had flowed again into these tanks, the water pressure on the weakened metal had forced as many holes as in a colander.

There was no question of summoning a plumber. He would certainly have recommended a new tank, which with all the necessary pipes and fittings would have run into hundreds of pounds. We would have to bodge something up for ourselves. Unfortunately Tom was in no state to do this. He was in bed, immobile, after pulling a muscle in his neck whilst jumping a horse. Nor was he likely to be fit enough for several weeks to tackle a long and arduous job like mending a 1000-gallon tank. The only thing to do, he said, was to switch the pump on for five minutes three or four times a day. That would give the hot-water cistern in the house the opportunity to fill up, and give the cattle in the barn a chance to have a drink before it all dripped away.

We eased our worries about this latest set-back by following the sad and continuing tale of the pipeline at Ross. It is amazing how a knowledge that others have problems can help one sustain one's own. It was clear from the papers that this pipeline was making little progress. A public inquiry was being held to hear objections to the scheme. The serious objectors who opposed it on environmental grounds had faded from the picture. Left alone on the stage was a group which was merely using the inquiry as a platform to voice their long-standing complaint about the quality and purity of the cocoa-coloured water which came out of their taps. This group had never intended to delay a supply to others who had no water at all, but democracy had to be seen to be done. So the inquiry ground on, hearing all these objections before it finally approved the scheme. But when the scheme finally did get under way, the authority showed real enterprise, and put together what was described as 'a scratch assembly of an entire new waterworks'.

And from the Water Authority came another warning about shortages – the direst yet. Herefordshire, they stressed, was now facing the worst drought of the century. The authority then went on to say, in terms which certainly reflected our experience, that the main victims would be those who relied on private underground sources of water. Large areas of the county were still drawing water from this type of supply, which would, in more and more places, inevitably run dry. Those in the lowlands were at the greatest risk. The authority advised people on wells and bore-holes to get linked to the mains as soon as possible.

In the second week of March the weather taunted us again with two brief showers. My parents came to stay for the weekend, to help us get the garden dug and the vegetables planted. Though they are the sort of people who can put up with the odd inconvenience like no water, the farm was bedlam with five people and a baby in the house. The rusted cistern was leaking more than ever, and just could not carry the burden. I was swamped with requests for hot rainwater for shaving and washing. The lavatory floor was awash where people had misfired emptying buckets into the cistern – a fine art until you master it – and the bucket of precious nappy soak solution was liable to disappear, flushed down the lavatory by mistake.

Tom and I had our first night out for over six months, and it was an unmitigated disaster. Tired and cold we sat for hours in the dreary Nissen hut annex which housed a local hotel's 'Nite Spot'. We had not realized how bone-weary we were, after these months of supporting the extra burdens of hauling, carrying, conserving and worrying over water. Everyone else in the bar was in fine form. They were downing spirits, mainly terrible mixtures like gin and coke, as if Prohibition was about to be introduced. They set about cheering us up, even though we were obviously dull dogs missing out on half the rounds, which kept appearing at five-minute intervals. Even so we must have had eight or nine Scotches apiece. It left us dizzily miserable, as we waited for the cabaret. Two hours late the star performer minced onto the stage – a former policeman who had undergone a sex change operation in Casablanca. It was all too much.

At seven o'clock the next morning, after five hours of disturbed sleep, I crawled out of bed to find there was not a drop of water on the farm. Not even any rainwater. Nothing for the stock, for a wash, for a cup of tea. To struggle through the mud of the dew-pond in the hope of gathering a bucketful or two was a nightmare prospect. It was far too early to disturb our neighbours by seeking to draw a load of water. For the first time that winter I felt I simply could not cope any further. I sat down at the kitchen table and wept. My father appeared and, full of concern, remembered he had half a crate of Malvern water in the boot of his car.

We had always laughed at his distrust of water supplies in the countryside. Never again. He made a pot of tea, and helped us feed the cattle. They ate heartily enough, even if they would have to wait until later for a drink. After breakfast I crept back into bed and left everyone else to do the work while my hangover ran its course.

In the afternoon Tom and I planned to go out for a couple of hours. As I was performing the unusual feat of putting on a skirt there was the sound of a car engine dying in the yard, followed by furious barking.

It was the vicar. Only divine intervention – the alsatian spotted a cat – prevented him being eaten alive before he reached the front door. While I shut up the dog, Tom steered the vicar round the back, explaining that there was no entry through the front door because we had sealed it up with sticky tape to keep out the draughts.

The vicar was concerned, understandably, for us to come to the family service he had just instituted. I was about to explain how the drought had robbed us of time to do anything more than just survive, that we were hit not just by shortage of water, but by lack of water, when I realized words could not do the job. Unless one had experienced directly the constant heavy drag on one's energies, day after day, I felt it was not possible to appreciate the huge gulf which extended between having, and not having, enough water. I thought about trying a light-hearted plea that he might persuade the Almighty to reconnect our water supply, but decided that silence was the better course.

But the vicar was cheerful and heartening, and we had enough water to offer him a cup of tea. Perhaps it was just my hangover was curing itself, but I suddenly felt more optimistic, as if we were turning one corner at least in our long drought journey.

And events supported that optimism. Tom recovered, and fixed the leaking tank. Then, miraculously, it rained, not just once, but off and on for the next three weeks, as if the weather had suddenly come to its senses at last. By the end of the month the well was half full. We peered down at its glinting surface each morning with delight. Once again we were ready to believe that the worst was over.

Financially, too, our prospects were beginning to look rosier. On the cattle market prices had been rising steadily during the winter months, as the shortages caused by the massive calf slaughterings of the previous year began to be felt. From £19 a hundredweight in the autumn, the price for store cattle – those not yet ready for the butcher – had inched up to £23, and now leapt to £28. We had fortunately stocked up with calves when the market had been at rock bottom in the winter of 1974–5. Now, remembering the extent to which Britain's potential cattle numbers had been reduced, we reckoned the price was bound to go even higher. As soon as the well was producing ample supplies of water Tom bought another dozen medium-sized cattle. We had no proper pens to put them into for the six weeks before we could turn out the stock. We had cattle filling every loose box and shed on the place. In the early morning, when they gazed out across the yard over every gate and above every loose-box door, the place looked like Noah's Ark. And by April the price had risen to £33 a hundredweight. We still had no money in the bank, but the important thing was that we felt a lot better off.

As March continued the weather became perfect for farmers. All around us was the throb of tractors as farmers planted their spring corn and root crops in the best conditions for many years. They certainly suited one local farmer, Stan Phillips. He was a land-hungry man (indeed, what farmer is not?), forever trying to increase his eighty-acre holding. Now he had succeeded in 'borrowing' two half-acre plots, overgrown vegetable gardens behind some cottages belonging to retired city-dwellers. In these minute fields he had planted potatoes, an act which could have carried him into conflict with the Potato Marketing Board. They operate a rigorous quota system to limit acreage, and whether Stan Phillips had exceeded his acreage or not turned on a fine point of interpretation of the rules as to whether these could strictly be classified as his potatoes. But the village found it a good ploy not to give him the benefit of the doubt. It became common practice to say when he was within earshot: 'Yer see the Potato Marketing Board helicopter today? Him be looking for illegal taters.'

Phillips would laugh it off, but with a real concern under the laughter. He had the farmer's inbuilt wariness of authority, that blind and capricious force which overhangs the countryside and which can cause endless trouble if aroused. But he had the last laugh on us. By October those potatoes were worth £2000 an acre.

At the end of March we took stock of the situation, not without confidence. We had survived for almost six months without an adequate water supply. Apart from a few septic scratches we seemed none the worse for it. We had still to face the summer. The well was half full, but I bet Tom it would not last beyond the end of May. The dew-pond would have to see us through the rest of the summer as a supply for the livestock. Our big worry was supplies for the house. Dirt may be unpleasant, but will not kill you in the winter. In the summer, particularly on a livestock farm, it could clearly cause great problems.

6. April 1976

April, according to the poets, the meteorologists and tradition, is the month when gentle showers of rain combine with outbursts of sun to trigger off the cycle of summer growth in Britain. But since 1971 April has been a dry, cold month with the vivification of the soil held entombed in the hard ground. April 1976 followed the pattern of previous years, except that it was a little warmer. Of those famous April showers we saw nothing at all; rain was limited to two days of intermittent drizzle in the middle of the month.

On our farm, as on many livestock farms, April is officially the last month of winter – winter being the time when the stock are housed inside. On some days it seems to be the longest month of the year. Corn and fodder stocks run critically low. We have been feeding the cattle, morning and night, for five months. The few remaining weeks of this burden seem an eternity. All around us are the harbingers of spring. The starkness of winter gives way to a softer outlook. The sun, climbing steadily in the sky, highlights the hedgerows pricked with pinpoints of green. The naked trees look almost furry with their full ripe leaf buds. The banks of the lane are bright with celandines and the grass grows visibly greener every day, particularly on the roadside verges where the new growth throws off the brown dredging of mud sprayed on it incessantly in winter by passing vehicles.

At times we are tempted to turn the stock out early, and have done with winter chores. But we know that could be disastrous. Cattle do not thrive on wet, lush grass, nor on the sudden frosts which April can bring. On our farm the grass is always a week or two later than on farms on a lower contour near the village. A sudden cold spell can stop the growth altogether for weeks at a time. That can set off a vicious circle: the cattle run short of grass, and have to be turned onto leys which are still only partially grown; there they start eating all the new shoots, as these appear; before you know it you can be short of grass all summer. In previous years we had learned that patience pays: the extra cost of keeping the cattle inside during April was repaid three times over in the extra hay we were able to get off the pastures.

In other ways spring is very much with us in April. The show-jumping season gets underway and there is the land to attend to. Even on a grass farm there is a lot to do: harrowing, rolling and fertilizer-spreading for a strong, early growth of grass. Anyone watching a tractor trundle round a field dragging a set of chain harrows might think it a dreary way to spend an afternoon. Far from it; in the early spring there are few things to equal the exhilarating sensation of lurching across the bumpy ridge and furrow pasture with the harrows scouring out the dead winter grass and smashing all the unsightly cow pats and molehills to bits. From the vantage point of the tractor seat there are all the signs of life beginning to stir again after the long winter break.

The countryside seems full of birds in April, perhaps because there is no foliage to conceal them on the trees and hedgerows and no long grass to hide them on the ground. This April the ground seemed to vibrate with lapwings, their big black combs silhouetted against the bare plough. Every now and then a group of them would take to the air and stage the most incredible display flights with wildly erratic swoops and sudden headlong plunges towards the ground.

On the ridge by the pond a party of curlews was making a rare visit. Though their colouring is far from spectacular, their mere size – they are the largest wading birds in Europe – makes them appear exotic. Occasionally we would hear the call of an early cuckoo – such a heartening sound in early spring, but such a maddeningly monotonous sound by late summer that some-times we itch to grab a couple of twelve-bores and silence it for ever.

Despite the extra work the month always brings, April 1976 was a time of respite on our farm. The March rain had left us with enough water for both the stock and the house so for once we were able to lead a fairly normal life.

From other areas, too, the April news in the papers was hopeful. The long-suffering people of the hamlet of Newton were told that the local district council was going to guarantee £10000 a year to underwrite a mains connection. A week later the first water from the emergency pipeline from the River Wye had begun to trickle in to our fellow sufferers, the water-starved people of Howle Hill, near Ross. We gave them a distant cheer.

Around the farm spring revealed more and more signs of the way the peculiar weather of the past eighteen months was upsetting the normal pattern of the wildlife. The first thing we noticed was that the cattle were suffering from an ailment known as New Forest eye disease. This is thought to be carried by flies, and usually strikes only in July and August in hot dry summers. We were hit by it in April, and it was to infect and re-infect the cattle all summer.

Then the chickens began to go AWOL or, as it turned out, missing presumed dead. Those fifth columnists in Britain's battle against rabies – the foxes – were experiencing a population increase of unprecedented proportions. Two mild winters in succession had had a dramatic effect on the mortality rate among young cubs. At the same time the exceptionally dry weather had hampered the foxhounds. Even though fewer hunting days had been lost because of mist or ice, on many days the scent had been poor. Huntsmen in the south of England agreed that the season's kill had been no better than average, even though foxes had been more numerous.

Now, after an unexacting winter, the vixens were producing their litters earlier than usual – hence the decimation of the free-range hen population, in the absence of the more accessible titbits like pheasants' eggs.

Down at the local poultry farm they were delighted. The sudden fecundity of the fox population was promoting a brisk trade in replacement hens. But the farm itself also had its problems from fertile wildlife. Badgers, frantic for food to feed their extra young, stood on their hind legs and rattled the wire of the cages at night. It frightened the pullets so much they promptly stopped laying.

Other aspects of our self-sufficiency enterprises were also suffering. An army of rabbits, undeterred by the wire netting around the vegetable garden, tunnelled in daily to wipe out any trace of the young lettuces and cabbages we planted. Surrounded and indeed invaded by so much fauna, the vegetable garden looked distinctly short of useful flora. It became a constant irritation. Like everything else on the farm it had run to seed by the time we moved in. During the past two years, aided by much skill and labour from my mother, we had managed to wrench half of it back from nature's tenacious grasp. The other half was a wilderness of grass that grew faster and thicker then it ever did in the fields. At one time we had been so short of grazing on the farm that we had lodged Angel, our affectionate but cantankerous house-cow, in there for a week.

Gazing at the derelict mess in the middle of April, it seemed to me unforgivable to waste such valuable space when in the coming months we might need every cabbage and potato we could grow. So we pitched in with forks and spent every spare moment for the next three weeks digging. It turned out to be one of the hardest, guttiest jobs we had to do on the farm. But when it was finished and the garden was planted with potatoes and hot-weather vegetables like courgettes, sweet corn and tomatoes, it was well worth the trouble. Like Phillips's potato plots it paid off handsomely.

While we were digging away warnings of a severe drought came thick and fast. First the Ministry of Agriculture urged farmers to check all water-pipes and connections for leaks. The ministry took the unprecedented step of asking stockmen to wash down cow sheds with buckets instead of hose-pipes. Finally it suggested that people with private supplies should try to store as much water as possible.

By the end of April the drought was news even outside the stricken areas. Supplies to the industrial towns of south Wales were endangered as the Brecon reservoirs dried up, and photographs of the cracked mud flats of these reservoirs began to appear in the newspapers and on television. Pitsford reservoir in Northamptonshire became a favourite for the camermen when the supplies in it became so low that it became possible to drive across it along a road which had disappeared when the valley had first been flooded.

It was now that the division of Britain into two nations – those with plenty of water, and those facing real shortages – began to develop. North of a line from the Wash to Pembrokeshire the country was relatively unaffected. There had been a reasonable amount of rain there throughout the winter, and Scotland indeed was to face a summer of abundant rainfall. South of this line the effects were patchy, but where the drought was hitting it was hitting hard. Wiltshire was severely short of water, as was south Wales, and East Anglia and the east Midlands. Devon, too, began to feature as a threatened area. Stand-pipes such as had been used for emergency supplies in the blitz were being ordered by local authorities, and the water authorities were tracking down tankers for use if the piped supplies failed.

At this stage Herefordshire was not publicized as an endangered region despite the shortage in some of its territory. It did not get into the national news until late in the summer. Indeed it was to escape, by some quirk of the media, much of the publicity about the drought. This was not due to reticence on the part of the local Water Authority. They were loud in their warnings. In the south of the county rainfall for the first three months of 1976 had been only half the normal level. This came on top of a loss of twenty-eight inches – equivalent to a full year's rainfall – over the past five years. The Herefordshire divisional manager of the Water Authority, Mr Bill Austin, spoke in terms which would in the past have been regarded as the doomsday imaginings of an hysterical environmentalist. 'This is the drought of the century. We have not got the water to cope with the demand. There will be rationing before the summer.'

Worried officials called for stronger methods for conserving supplies. A ban on the use of hose-pipes for car washing, and on garden sprinklers had existed since last summer. Now people were urged to put half a brick into their lavatory cisterns. New wells were being sunk in Herefordshire for the first time for over one hundred years.

The market was buzzing with rumours. Dealers from Cardiff predicted that their city would soon be on a three-day working week to conserve supplies. Horticulturalists were filled with alarm when rumour had it that their business would be classed as non-essential, and that their supplies would be rationed. Farmers noted that agriculture was regarded as an essential industry, but became increasingly suspicious that when it came to the crunch they might be hard hit all the same. Farming journals were full of warnings of the dangers to cattle if we had dry weather right through the summer.

Perhaps the farming community took it all too gloomily. But stock farmers carry a responsibility for the lives of many animals, animals utterly dependent upon their owners for food and water. This was a different, more urgent anxiety than that which obsessed the arable farmer. His crops might die, but they were not going to suffer in the process in the way which livestock would suffer. Warnings which were to much of the country a warning of difficulties or discomforts were to us warnings of a disaster which looked only too real. If we were heading for the worst drought for 200 years, we were heading for it in a country with a population five times greater than it was then. In the eighteenth century, too, industry was in its infancy. Water used in the home was restricted by the fact that every drop had to be carried in from outside. People did not have a daily soak in a deep bath, nor flush lavatories nor use automatic washing machines that rinse each load of clothes six times.

How to manage if water rationing was introduced became a central topic of conversation. Farmers' wives who had lived for years without tap water took a certain grim satisfaction in anticipating the reactions of the city dwellers. At supper on Easter Monday one of my neighbours, Sue Hopkins, voiced what was a widely held view.

'Today's younger townspeople have never known what it was like to be without water from the tap. When I was a kid if you wanted to go to the toilet you had to go outside to the privy. We had one bath a week, on Fridays, in a tin tub in front of the kitchen fire. All of us took it in turns in the same water.

'Every drop we used had to be carried from outside – so you made sure you didn't use more than you had to. In the summer we kids had to carry drinking water up from the well in the fields when the one by the house ran out. These people in the towns don't know how lucky they are. My husband's sister often leaves the tap on just because she likes the sound of running water.'

On the farm we were taking our own precautions. Tom went off to a farm sale and returned with several hundred yards of plastic hose-pipe and a 500-gallon water trough. We could see our major problem in a dry summer would be how to get water to the stock in the fields. Apart from the pasture with the dew-pond and the one with its own well, all the other fields had water troughs fed from the well in the kitchen garden. No water in the well meant no water in the fields.

We planned, therefore, to use our newly acquired hose-pipe to run water directly from the dew-pond to any pastures lacking their usual water supply. The only snag with this was that permanent troughs, which normally filled automatically, held only forty gallons and it would mean replenishing them as often as ten times a day. That was where the new 500-gallon trough came in. We intended to put it in whichever field the cattle were in, shifting it with the tractor every time we moved the stock to fresh grazing. Water from the dew-pond could then be pumped directly into the trough only once a day or even less often.

We also wanted to ensure that the grass we had lasted as long as possible in case the dry spell continued into the summer and prevented any further growth. Tom set to and built a series of fences which divided up the twelve-acre field at the front of the farm into four-acre paddocks. It meant however that we had three gates to open and close every time we went down the drive, and we cussed the inconvenience loudly at first.

But though we went through the motions of making contingency plans we could not quite believe that there really would be another summer like the one the previous year. The idea of two scorching summers in a row in Britain seemed almost laughable.

Yet we joined with our farming friends in making grim predictions of how our neighbours were bound to go bankrupt. We had a visit from one of the most pessimistic of these Cassandras one sunny day towards the end of April. His name was Don Parker; he was a likable, lively young farmer who was adept at the local sport of teasing his fellow farmers. It was all done with polite diffidence, and we took care to react with extreme offhandedness. But afterwards his mild observations seemed to take root in our minds, and to flower into serious misgivings.

We would sit by the fire after he had left chewing over his comments. As neither of us were lifelong farmers we had learnt some valuable lessons from our neighbours. At the same time we realized our ignorance made us a prime target for their leg-pulling. Some of Don Parker's jokes were obvious enough. On one occasion he had told me I was milking the cow from the wrong side and for a second or two I believed him. But often he left us perplexed. Another time, for instance, he told us the tyres on the tractor were the wrong way round for muck-spreading. That really floored us. We stared hard at the tyres with the dawning realization that we had no idea there was a 'right way' and 'wrong way' round for tyres for that particular job. As it turned out, there is a 'right' way and our tractor tyres did have the treads facing in the correct direction.

Don Parker's most recent remark, made on a visit the previous month, was still causing us some concern. He reckoned a red and white calf we had bought in the market had some black hairs in its coat. Now buying calves in the market is fraught with pitfalls, particularly for the inexperienced. One was that a calf from a Jersey cow by a Hereford bull could easily resemble its red and white sire for the first three months or so. But from then on instead of growing large and fat its mother's characteristics would come through and it became fine-boned and thin and useless for beef. Time proved Don Parker to be correct in this case.

But we enjoyed these battles of wits, even if he brought with him an unruly collie which was adept at leaping through our car windows and smothering the seats in mud. On this occasion when Don appeared we had been forewarned. We knew that he was trying to get rid of a tump of mangolds which were beginning to rot by his farm buildings.

'Nice lot of young cattle you've got there,' he said, starting his sales pitch.

'Mm,' I said. 'They could be a bit bigger.'

He appeared to ruminate for several minutes. 'What they getting – barley? Mm. They need something more. Something nice and juicy. They like that. A bit of silage – or better still, some roots.'

'What they really need,' I replied, tongue firmly in cheek, 'are some mangolds. Just the job.'

There was another two-minute silence as we studied the cattle. 'I could let you have some mangolds. I've put some by. You could have the lot for twelve pounds a ton.'

After three years in Herefordshire I was taken aback that we

C

were still regarded as greenhorns. I appeared to ponder his offer, and then replied, 'You could get that for them in Hereford market. All you'd have to do would be to load them onto a trailer – and of course it's a long cold drive there and back on a tractor in this weather. We'll take them off you for a few quid, but you've tried the wrong people for twelve pounds a ton.'

The smile never left his face, but his eyes narrowed. He savoured this kind of cut and thrust. He saw I was not likely to be shifted. In the event he did himself a favour by not selling us the mangolds because he was to need them for his own cattle that summer. He ended our discussion cheerfully. 'Ah well, you'll be turning them out in a day or two. No point spending money on extra feed.'

But he was not to let me off so lightly. A look of simulated concern spread over his features. 'How many you got? Fifty head! On forty acres! You'll not be making any hay then this year?'

'Fourteen acres,' I replied.

He became the very personification of doubt. 'Fourteen acres of hay! That's a lot to set aside when you'll need a lot of grass right away for fifty head, a lot of grass. If it's a dry summer again you'll be in trouble. Yes, I can see you might be very short of grass. If it was me I'd sell half of them now. The market's right up. Yes, I should sell.'

We shrugged off these predictions, and held to our plan to make hay from fourteen of our scarce acres. We did not sell our cattle and Don Parker never did sell his mangolds. He fed most of them to his young cattle and the rest rotted in the heap. But by the end of the month it began to look as if Parker had been horribly realistic. The rain held off, and the grass growth was a good three weeks behind normal. As we walked through the thin stalky grass it was clear that unless it rained within ten days we would be in trouble. We had enough grazing for only six weeks. After that we would face the choice of selling half of the cattle, or turning them into the fields set aside for hay.

A third possibility – to keep them in their winter quarters for another two or three weeks – was out of the question. We had enough corn and fodder for only five more days. To buy in extra supplies at the end of the winter season would have been prohibitively expensive. And to complete our dilemma the well was falling fast. It was only just providing enough water for the stock.

A friend who works in Paris came to stay for a few days. For the first time we learnt that the drought was not limited to southern Britain. In France, he told us, farmers in the more isolated areas were talking about slaughtering their cows because they were running short of drinking water. Without enough water a cow's milk yield drops and it can take a long time to recover. Then from economic necessity the cow has to go because it would cost more to feed it than to sell it and replace it when water supplies returned to normal.

Our friend tackled the problem of the drought on conventional business lines. His solutions were logical but impractical. One suggestion was that we should buy an ex-army tanker to cart water. The only flaw in that idea was that it would have cost as much, if not more, as having a connection to the mains.

To overcome the lack of grass he recommended zero grazing – a system used extensively in America but only on a limited scale in Britain. It involves keeping the cattle permanently in sheds and cutting the grass several times a day and taking it to them. On a farm with the necessary equipment and the right buildings it is a viable system. But to try it on forty acres with unsophisticated machinery you would have to be crazy.

Other farmers in the area were by now equally worried. The newspapers were full of another subject. Would the trade unions accept the Chancellor's pay policy? Don Parker put our farming viewpoint in a nutshell. 'There won't be any food to buy with their extra four per cent, or the eighty pounds a week they earn now if this weather goes on.'

The potato shortage had already demonstrated how much the success of farming in Britain depends on our much-lamented damp climate. After twelve dry months another rainless six weeks would threaten almost every crop grown in the country – wheat, barley for beer and animal feed, vegetables, and of course grass – grass for fodder, cows, beef, sheep.

I rang the meteorological office almost every day. Then at long last on 29 April the duty officer said the picture was definitely changing and rain should arrive in the next three days. On 2 May, as I was driving home from town with a box of lettuce plants to replace the ones that had provided breakfast that morning for the rabbits, dark heavy clouds began to gather on the horizon. Rain, in great handfuls, hit the windscreen. We had bought the car six weeks before and I realized I had no idea how the windscreen wipers worked.

7. May 1976

In May, for the first time during the fifteen months of the drought, the weather was kind to us. Gentle refreshing spring showers with sunny spells were the meteorological programme for the month. Other parts of the country were less fortunate. On the desiccated earth of the south-west, south-east and of East Anglia, the rainfall was slight. In the eastern counties what little rain fell soon drained away through the fine sandy soil. Many farmers in those areas were to suffer the crop failures that we had feared in April.

In the west Midlands we were extraordinarily lucky. In Herefordshire the rich heavy soil retained the moisture well, until the June heat-wave scorched the life out of the countryside. Spring-planted crops shot up. Root vegetables got a good start which enabled them, when the real drought struck, to put down long tap roots to the moisture far below the surface. The autumn-sown corn revived and grew strong and tall, promising a heavy straw harvest if nothing else.

And there was the grass. If it did not quite grow under our feet, it certainly shot up overnight. The fields were heavy with it: a dark green sea of lushness that rippled in the evening breeze. Everywhere you looked there was a sumptuous, almost over-indulgent display of wild flowers. It was a great year for the humble dandelion. Roadside verges were pure gold. In the fields the dandelions grew so thickly that pastures appeared to have been sown with mustard rather than with grass. Where dandelions did not dominate the scene, buttercups, daisies, speedwell, vetches, clover, milkworts, primroses and cowslips flowered in a frenzy, as if nature was forewarned that it was to have barely six weeks in which to complete its entire summer cycle.

On 3 May we finally turned our cattle out to grass for the summer. To me 'turn-out day' is the best in the whole farming calendar. The repetitive winter chores are over for six whole months. The long morning and evening ritual of feeding and watering and forking-out is ended. Now we can watch the cattle eat in the fields and put on weight. There is plenty of other work for us to do in the summer, but it is varied and in the open. Often we do not finish for the day until the late dusk sets in, but the work is more satisfying. At the end of the day there is something to show for it – a field of hay baled, a barn full of straw.

By the middle of May the grass was up to our knees, and we began to turn our thoughts to haymaking. Through an advertisement in the local paper, offering a hay turner for sale, we made an expedition to a farm in south Worcestershire. It gave us a glimpse of a farming era that is passing into history. It was a livestock holding of the kind that had been common before the war – indeed our own farm had been run on similar lines for many years. In the days before churns and bottling plants and milk roundsmen in electric floats, liquid milk production was mainly confined to farms near towns. The more isolated farms produced that luxury product – butter – which was taken into the nearest market town once a week to be sold.

Most butter-makers were small farmers with ten or fifteen cows and some calves or pigs which were fed on the skim milk left after the cream had been removed. The butter bore little resemblance to the uniform product churned out today by the thousands of tons. Each farm's butter had its own unique taste and colour. Even neighbours produced vastly different products. One farm might be famous for its buttercup yellow colour; down the road it could invariably turn out a lighter creamier colour. This was largely because most fields in those days were permanent pastures with their own individual combination of grasses and herbs in the turf.

Taste and keeping qualities also owed much to the skill of the butter-maker – usually the farmer's wife. Though people claim butter can be made quickly and easily with an electric mixer, real butter-making is a fine art. After the cream is separated it is tipped into the churn along with a little cream kept back from the previous week. The trick is to keep back the cream from the right day so it is 'ripe' and not sour. Then comes all the hard work, turning and turning the paddle until finally the butter forms in granules. In hot weather it can take hours and when thunder is in the air the butter can 'go to sleep' sticking to the side of the churn so the paddle swings round ineffectively. The butter is 'woken up' by putting two spoons in the churn.

The farm we visited had a low half-timbered black and white farmhouse crouched in a dell which was surrounded by ancient orchards and an immaculate kitchen garden. It was as though the weight of its years was forcing it into its very foundations. In the orchard was an amazing variety of farming tackle which appeared to have been left to take root. Freeing the hay turner from the tenacious mat of grass that anchored it to the ground took three of us the best part of half an hour, so we were more than grateful when the old farmer invited us inside for a glass of elderflower wine. To reach the kitchen door we had to wade through a menagerie of every type of domestic fowl that must exist in Britain – chickens, bantams, ducks, muscovy ducks, geese, turkeys, guinea fowl and several I could not identify. The farmer dismissed this unusual collection with, 'What don't pay, others will.'

Negotiating our way through a pile of firewood, a stack of cardboard boxes and a mountain of Wellington boots by the door, we nearly tripped over a bucket half-full of eggs every bit as varied as their antecedents. 'Do you sell these?' asked Tom indicating the bucket. Who the hell, we were thinking, would want those enormous turkey eggs?

The old man looked at us as though we were mad. 'Aaat, aaar. There's a good demand for all eggs in Tenbury market.'

We groped our way through the gloomy passage to the kitchen. It had once been large and spacious, but over the years it had shrunk. Stacks of papers, bills, spent cartridges, tins and tubes of veterinary products and other impedimenta of living had piled up round the walls and confined the family to a small fairly clear space by the range. It was bounded by two ancient and collapsing sofas, one occupied by a family of cats. Arising in triumph from the mess on the far side of the room was a television set – the kind with a large cabinet and small screen produced in the early 1950s.

There were only two concessions to the 1970s: one was an enormous commercial freezer packed with home-grown vegetables and home-made butter. The other was a fridge – a great improvement on the traditional way of cooling cream in hot weather, which involved suspending it in a bucket down a deep well.

We sat down, or rather collapsed, on the unoccupied sofa and the wine was produced in a cracked earthenware jug. Pale yellow, light and dry, yet thirst-quenching at the same time, it was by far the best home-made wine I have ever tasted. Conversation started tentatively with the weather. At first the old man was uncommunicative but the wine obviously oiled his vocal chords, for after a few minutes he was away.

'Never known nothing like it. Been here sixty years. Me and the missus. We thought we'd seen it all. Course we've known it hot before and floods! Do you remember, missus? When the snow melted in 1947 the water was three-foot deep in the house. We had to sit in the rainwater tank and paddle it across the yard to the toilet.

'It used to change then. But this last year or two it sets in, like. Never remember a summer like last year nor a winter as dry as the one that's just been.'

He paused and took a long draught of elderflower wine.

'If it's hot again lot of folks will be in trouble. It's all these new methods. Never did hold with them. Take all this draining people is mad about – government even pays 'em to do it. You got a marshy field. Course you can't put your stock in it in early spring. But then if it's dry later on you've got a bit of grass put by when the rest of the farm's as bare as a badger's arse.' He laughed heartily and took another drink.

'Then there's the government. Always poking its nose in. Do this, fill in that. But if you want something you've a right to then they don't want to know. Piss off, they say, I'm too busy poking my nose into something else.

'Like the water people. What are they in it for if it's not to provide water? We're on the mains. But up the hill they're on a well. It's dry now, and they want the mains. But the people say no new connections, go and draw water from the river if you're short. It's not right, cattle going short while other folks have as much water as they want.'

With that he subsided into silence again. Tom produced his cheque-book to settle for the hay turner. Another round of elderflower wine sealed the deal. Before we left Tom bought a pound of butter from the 'missus'. He thought it was marvellous. But I, perhaps too much used to the bland axle grease of modern butter, found it rich and rancid. We still have half a pound in a corner of our freezer.

The May rain helped our crops, but it came too late to stave off the real water shortage. From the end of April onwards there was no hope that rainwater would filter through the ground and get to the subterranean reservoirs, or flow into the sluggish streams which had once been the great rivers of Britain. The Government was not unduly perturbed by the situation. Mr John Silkin, Minister for Planning and Local Government, told the Commons: 'The immediate situation is under control given sensible use by consumers.' He went on to say that the water authorities expected to avoid major interruptions. That was on the assumption there would be normal rainfall in the summer.

Nevertheless, appeals from the water authorities in the water-starved areas became louder and more frequent. People were urged to use waste bath-water for washing cars and watering gardens. An ingenious gardener wrote to the papers recommending the use of a Wellington boot, slipped over the bottom of the drain pipe, and with a hole cut in the toe, as a means of steering your bath water into a hose-pipe. One local authority made half bricks available for lavatory cisterns. Another suggested you should fill an eight-ounce coffee jar with pebbles for the same purpose. A plastic bag filled with water and tied inside the cistern had its advocates. The message seemed to be: save a pint a pull and keep the reservoirs full.

There were demands that washing machines should be banned. Some models could use as much as fifty gallons of water a load. Posters began to appear in towns setting out measures to conserve water. Tap washers in particular should be checked. 'Every drip prolongs the drought', was its slogan. Severely affected areas had warning signs on their borders. These showed a picture of dry, cracked earth and the words, 'You are now entering a drought area'. It sent a chill down our spines.

Television was in full cry now about the drought. Just how serious it was likely to be was outlined by a BBC documentary

screened towards the end of May. At the time, though, its con-
clusions seemed a bit far-fetched, even to us. But the programme
certainly had the effect of sparking off new talk about the water
shortage in Micklebury. Harry, our Welsh singing postman, was
snorting with disgust the following morning. 'They're all talking
about it now, but it's only because the people in the towns may
be rationed. I've known of people round here who haven't had
any water – old people too, you know – readily available since
last summer. And no one wants to know, no one wants to do
anything about it. They tell them to go and have a bath with their
relatives.'

He snorted again and I added my heartfelt agreement. 'I know
just what you mean,' I said. And so I did.

His sentiments were echoed by Anne Summers, a farmer's
daughter from Micklebury who had begun to help me in the
house once a week that spring. She had two outstanding characteristics: she was an invaluable purveyor of neighbourhood news,
and she always dressed immaculately – she would not have been
out of place on the Champs-Élysées.

Hardly had Harry bolted off in his red van when Anne arrived
shaking with vexation. 'As soon as the people in the towns might
go short everyone makes a terrible fuss. But the country folk,
they don't matter. They think: "Oh, country people will manage,
they always do."

'D'you know the Harrisons – I go there on Tuesday mornings –
have had no water since this time last year? They have a tanker
deliver it. And it's terribly expensive. The driver was telling them
it's lucky they ran out so early on because so many people want
water now they won't be able to get round all of them.'

Comments like these presaged the beginning of a contempt of
'townies' that was to develop during that harsh summer. Most of
the time country people ignore or tolerate people from the towns.
They envy their higher wages but not the frenetic pace of life
that goes with them. The country attitude is: 'If that's what they
want, they're welcome to it, but we wouldn't want to live like
that.'

This traditional tolerance had already worn a bit thin by the
start of the summer. Farmers, in particular, were growing increasingly irritated by the distorted image they had gained. If he
wasn't the simple rustic of the television commercials he was seen

as a well-dressed man in tweeds always bemoaning the fact he was on the verge of bankruptcy. He was the possessor of a Range Rover and two other cars and had his pockets stuffed with readies squeezed out of impoverished housewives by high prices and the taxation that provided agriculture with huge subsidies.

The truth was very different, at least for livestock farmers. The collapse of the livestock market in 1974 followed by the drought in 1975 had saddled many of them with crushing overdrafts. Most of the farmers' wives around Micklebury now went out to work – in the fields, in factories, in offices, as cleaners, as teachers. Of those who stayed at home, many worked full-time on the farm releasing their husbands to work on contract on larger farms. And in the previous two years an epidemic of 'Bed and Breakfast' signs had appeared.

My neighbour, Sue Hopkins, worked shifts in the local factory – one week 6 a.m. till 2 p.m., the next 2 p.m. till 10 p.m. She also helped on the farm and coped with three school-aged sons. She became extremely aggravated by the attitude of her fellow workers. 'They think because you own a farm you must be rich. John will be wealthy when he's dead, but it's all on paper. There isn't enough money coming in to buy all the food we need and for things like new Wellingtons for the kids. But the people at the factory don't believe me when I say I have to go out to work, same as them.'

This resentment grew as time went on. As the summer progressed and farmers saw their grass and crops wither in the searing heat, complaints of high prices for the vegetables and meat they had managed to nurse to maturity added insult to injury. But all that was a long way away that green balmy spring.

8. June 1976

At the start of that long hot summer of 1976 there was no hint
of the devastation that nature was to produce in the coming
months. June is the month when Herefordshire comes into its
true glory. Looking over the valley to the Welsh hills we could
see the countryside unfold as a patchwork of variegated greens.
There was the pale jade of sprouting barley, the bottle green of
the young sugar beet and potatoes, the rich emerald of the wheat
and of the long lush grass which for generations has fattened the
red and white cattle that are probably better known than the
county itself. Here and there were smudges of brown topped by
splashes of sappy green – the dense copses of oak, beach and ash
once again in full summer regalia. The oaks had come into leaf
before the ash, promising a summer splash. But few people believe
this old rural omen. It is a rare spring when the ash beats the oak
to it.

In the farmyard our old friends, the swallows, were back. The
place always seems strangely empty in the winter without these
charming and friendly birds swooping and diving over the
buildings. As the summer weeks pass we watch the simple cycle
of their lives. First they renovate their nests – each pair always
returns to its own particular one. Next there is the cheep of chicks,
and yawning great beaks appear over the top of the nests as the
nestlings squawk endlessly at their harassed parents for food.
Then they venture into the outside world and with their parents
sit, blinking and nervous, on the electricity line that crosses the
farmyard. And within a few short weeks they are gone.

We entered the month in an optimistic mood. June showed
every sign, for the first few days, of living up to the long-range

weather forecast for the period – normal temperatures, normal rainfall. Most of the time the sky was filled with thick clouds heavy with rain. When the sun appeared, water sparkled and glinted in puddles, on roofs and as drops of dew on the lavish vegetation that had sprung up round the buildings. More water dripped luxuriously off the fresh green leaves on the gnarled old oaks and weather-beaten thorn trees in the pastures.

Even potato prices were falling at last. After being almost un-obtainable in April, except for a few old ones at 18p a pound, the new crop was coming into the shops and selling at about 12p a pound. However, not everyone was satisfied. I heard one old man ask the greengrocer for three pounds but then demand to know if they were English. When told they were Welsh, from Pembroke-shire, he replied: 'Oi'm not 'aving any of they ferrin buggers.' And he stomped out of the shop in disgust.

I had lost my bet, made with Tom back in March, that the well would be dry by the end of May. It came into June still holding a foot of water. Yet that was not enough for all the needs of the house. We rationed our flushing of the lavatory, and I started to take washing to the launderette again. Whenever I visited neigh-bours I took along the nappy bucket and a pile of hand-washing. Anne Summers also took a load of our washing home after her weekly visits to clean up the farmhouse.

We did have one serious problem – and it was one we had not anticipated. The level of our most reliable standby, the dew-pond, had dropped steadily during May and it was now falling alarming-ly fast. The water covered less than one third of its original area and every day seemed smaller. Mudbanks began to appear near the middle. It was looking less and less like a pond and more and more like a large puddle.

It seemed that by drawing off water at the rate of 500 gallons a day at one go for the cattle trough, we were upsetting the delicate and mysterious equilibrium of the dew-pond system. My theory was we were reducing the surface area of the pond quite signifi-cantly and thus the area attracting condensation from the dew. Cattle drinking from the pond would tend to drink little but often, and as long as the evening dews kept falling the surface area of the pond would remain fairly constant.

Another unexpected phenomenon, but a far more welcome one, was the quantity of grass on the farm. We already had fourteen acres set aside for hay and it looked as though we could get away with cutting another four. It was a tempting thought: the extra field would yield at least two tons to the acre. In hard cash that meant £400 worth of hay – a hefty windfall on a farm the size of ours. But there were two factors against it. For a start, if we had more grass than expected, then so would almost every other farmer – a situation which could push the hay price down from £50 a ton to below £30. And there was the risk of continuing drought. Another hot summer seemed highly unlikely at that stage, but the past six months had bred in us a peculiar caution.

The heat-wave the previous summer had come suddenly, at the end of the first week of June, after a cold May and, unbelievably, only seven days after some unseasonal snow showers. We were firmly convinced that the same thing could happen again. Reluctantly we decided an extra hay crop could be risky and that it was wiser to leave those four acres as grass for the cattle. With any luck we could take a late cut of hay at the end of July off one of the fields the cattle had already grazed.

June was only four days old when the weather dried up once again. After a year's experience we were past-masters at recognizing an imminent dry spell. The very air seemed to change as the humidity dropped, the water in the countryside evaporated overnight and the sounds of the trains and the traffic died.

All around us farmers were taking their first cut of silage and it was almost haymaking time. The grass growth was well advanced – another ten days and it would go to seed and lose some of its goodness. But to make good quality hay requires at least a week of fine weather. In a normal summer it is sometimes extraordinarily difficult to get it.

It is often said that farmers are never satisfied. And that was certainly true where we were concerned that June. After complaining about the lack of rain for the past twelve months we now wanted seven dry days on the trot in the next two weeks. We prevaricated. The meteorological office informed us it would be dry for the next three days and then more rain was expected.

Two days later the meteorological men were less confident. The rain was delayed for another couple of days, but the duty officer remarked sadly: 'It should rain then but going on the weather's form over the past twelve months we can't be sure about anything.'

The drought was exactly one year old.

It seemed an auspicious moment to start haymaking, so we rang up Rivers, the contractor, and he arranged to send up a local boy, called Ben David, to cut the hay the following day.

Ben arrived at five o'clock the next morning and proceeded to tear round the hay-field with the mower like a maniac. With his flaming red hair and bare back that became more salmon-coloured by the hour he began to look like a demented pixie trying to rev up enough speed to get the tractor airborne. As he bounced over the ridge and furrow ground there were moments when he nearly made it.

By dusk the hay was flat on the field. Surveying the field in the dying light of the June evening Tom and I felt the deep satisfaction that always envelopes us at the start of haymaking. It is the first actual product of our farming year and it marks the beginning of the period when we would reap some reward for the work we had put in during the winter and spring. It was a moment to savour; before us the dense unruly field of grass had been reduced to thick neat swards of hay in less than a day. On the soft evening breeze there was the heady smell of sappy grass.

But mowing day also signalled the start of the most nerve-racking week in the whole farming year. Once the grass is cut the fate of the hay is more or less sealed. An odd shower of rain does little harm but several days of persistent downpours can ruin the lot – and the farmer with it. On a small farm the margin between survival and bankruptcy is a narrow one determined as much by luck as by good management. A good hay crop is crucially important. Hay costing £50 a ton is too expensive to buy in from other farms.

Even the odd heavy shower can cause much consternation. In good weather the hay must be turned several times to 'make' it. Wet weather means more turning to dry out every blade and stalk. The longer the hay is out in the field the greater the chance of a long wet spell. And with every shower more and more of the nourishment is letched out of the hay.

The average British summer hardly gives the farmer a sporting chance; over the country as a whole the hay crop is of good quality only one year in every six.

The gods are normally with us for haymaking, though we had sampled the havoc the weather could produce the previous year.

Late in the evening the baler had broken down and a ton of hay had been left on the field to the mercy of a thunderstorm. Tom turned it the next day and it was ready to bale on the following one but then it rained again. This pattern of events was repeated for a fortnight. By the time we eventually managed to bale it all that was left was some fuzzy black stuff fit only for the bonfire.

Luckily we did not have time to read the newspapers that hay-making week in 1976. One of the undoubted advantages of our isolated farmhouse is that the papers are not delivered to the door. The milkman, who doubles up as newspaper boy, has no hope of making it up the drive in his electric float. Instead he leaves them at the sub post office in Micklebury. There the post-mistress, like many others in rural areas, presides over a dwindling empire. Once a budding retail entrepreneur, she has been forced by Value Added Tax, inflation and competition from a mobile shop to restrict her business to selling stamps and doling out pensions and social security payments. But her unpaid activities like newspaper collector, council rent collector and rural gazetteer for motorists, show no sign of a similar decline.

That week the newspapers were predicting an end to the dry spell with rain for the rest of the month. Above average rainfall, the meteorological office said, with no hope of a repetition of last year's flaming June. But Mother Nature had different ideas. Three days later the weather forecasters changed their tune abruptly. It was going to be dry for the next three or four days and it was doubtful if there would be any measurable rainfall after that in the foreseeable future.

Three days later Tom started to bale the hay. We stacked the bales into tumps of six behind the tractor. But until Tom had finished baling, the groom, Sarah, and I had no hope of getting the bales safely into the barn. Like most farms we have a hydraulic grab to lift the bales onto the trailer. But that worked only with the more powerful tractor, which was already being used with the baler. And the bales still had to be stacked by hand in the barn. Sarah and I were no Amazons. Pitching half-hundredweight bales up ten feet or more would have killed us.

By lunchtime the next day Tom was worried. He still had about 500 bales to do and he was convinced it was going to rain. The weathermen were still forecasting dry weather. High above the farmyard we could just make out the tiny specks of the swallows. Over the long dry months we had collected a mass of portents for the weather. But Tom had a new one. 'It's the flies around the horses' heads, they're like thick black clouds. That's a sure sign of rain,' he insisted. 'I'm going to ring the Davids boys and get them to lug the hay into the barns today.'

The Davids were duly summoned and stacked the first 1000 bales in the barn by ten that evening. It was a good yield – more than two and a half tons to the acre. Simon David, with an eye to another remunerative job, pointed to the twelve-acre field behind the barn. 'You going to skim that too?'

Tom shook his head. In answer to Simon's surprised expression I replied. 'You never know, if it doesn't rain for the rest of the summer at least we've got enough grass for the cattle until August.' The two brothers stopped drinking their coffee for a moment and stared at us as if we were slightly crazy.

Our anxiety over a possible drought did appear to be something of an obsession when Tom's instinct proved to be correct that night. Out of the blue, unheralded by the meteorological office or by any of the normal signs of the countryside, the rain came. The hay left outside did not suffer much as it was baled and stacked in tumps. After a morning's sunshine it was dry enough to put in the barn the next afternoon before the rain returned.

With the hay in the barns at least one of the summer's head-aches was over. Now all we had to put up with was the time-honoured tradition in Micklebury of a procession of neighbours coming to view it. First they would thrust their hands into the stack and withdraw a fistful and sniff it for sweetness. Then they would push an arm back into the stack and say: 'It's warming up a bit there, boy. I hope you've got this lot properly insured.' The implication was that the hay had been baled when damp and the whole stack was on the point of spontaneous combustion and our barn was about to go up in flames.

It rained on and off for the next few days. For once we were satisfied with the weather. It may not have helped the national water shortage but it delayed 'drying-up' day on our farm for several days by filling up the rainwater tanks.

But it could do little or nothing for the dew-pond. By that time there was absolutely no hope for it. The reason it was drying up was obvious: at night the temperature remained abnormally high, with the thermometer not dropping below 70 degrees Fahrenheit. There was simply no dew condensing to replenish supplies. At the current rate of evaporation it would last only another two weeks. After that we would have no water at all for our livestock. We rang the Water Authority. It seemed to have the situation organized this time, in contrast to the muddle in December. We could have a 1500-gallon tanker of water at forty-eight hours' notice. The cost would be between £10 and £15.

But the rain meant a welcome reprieve for a week or two. The weather forecasters had readopted their earlier prediction for June – or what was left of it. Some of the older farmers in Micklebury agreed with them.

Towards the end of the third week in June I bumped into one of them, Old Joady, in the post office. I never knew quite what to say when I met him because he was an eccentric character, who had taken on the role of the village seer, observing all, and given to confident yet cryptic utterances. He had a brown, bland face that did not betray his age; it could have been anything between forty and sixty.

He was in friendly form that morning.

'Got your hay in then?' The normal greeting in Micklebury in June. I nodded.

'Got a bit damp, I expect.' He looked highly sceptical when I replied it had not. Then he looked suddenly anxious.

'Still got to get mine. Twelve acres. Oi reckon we've 'ad the summer. Mmn, we've 'ad it.'

Joady was quite famous in the village for the misfortune which dogged his haymaking. He had a reputation for cutting his hay at the start of the wettest period of the summer.

'There used to be an old man round here,' he went on. 'Never went by them forecasts what you hear on the radio. But 'e always knew when rain was on the way. Never got a drop on his hay all the time he was farming. Know how he knew?

'By the moon. You look on the back of the Midland Seeds calendar. You know the one they give us Christmas. There's two Sunday moons in a row coming up and then one a fortnight later. Not been a Sunday moon for a twelvemonth or more. Now there's three in four weeks. Always a sign of unsettled weather. You see they'll be no more dry weather this summer.'

'I hope you are right,' I said – and I meant it.

Despite the rain we were still short of water for the house. We were hardened to this but we were jolted into realizing how much our former habits had altered by the arrival of yet another girl groom. Sarah had announced her intention of leaving the previous week, not because of the deprivations of the water shortage but because she had the chance of a job in a factory earning £55 a week. We were sorry to see her go but no farm or riding establishment, however successful, could pay a girl of eighteen that sort of wage. Her replacement, Morag, was a Scottish student doing a vacation job.

I gave her my set piece about the drought. 'There's a water shortage in this part of the world. Don't flush the loo unless you have to; I'm afraid it's only two tiny baths a week. Make sure all the taps are turned off tight. And whatever you do never, never leave the hose-pipe on.'

Tom hated this set speech of mine. 'I don't mind us going short but it's come to something when we have to ask people who work for us to adopt such filthy habits.'

Morag looked only mildly surprised. I presumed it was because the Scots often think that civilization stops at Hadrian's Wall and that our draconian water-saving measures were therefore no more unusual than many other manifestations of the English way of life.

Her surprise, it turned out, stemmed mainly from the fact that Scotland had received so much rain in the previous four weeks that the country was almost floating. But she understood the drought; the previous summer a hose-pipe ban had been introduced in Edinburgh, much to everyone's astonishment. And she was conscientious about sticking to the rules, apart from the odd lapse with the loose-box hose-pipe.

The day after Morag's arrival the real drought struck. Within forty-eight hours of Joady's astrological predictions the temperature leapt into the eighties. With sinking certainty we felt this was the start of a summer that would go down in history and one that we, personally, would never forget. We were in the front line. With fifty head of cattle, hardly any water and only grass for six weeks it was going to be a hard struggle.

Day by day the heat-wave in Britain built up. In Herefordshire the mercury crept up the thermometer: Wednesday, 23 June, 82 degrees; Thursday 80 degrees; Friday 87 degrees; Saturday 89 degrees; Sunday 91 degrees; Monday 91 degrees; Tuesday 90 degrees; Wednesday 90 degrees.

We started a work routine that was to last for the rest of the summer. We got up at five, began work at six and then, after a break for breakfast at eight, went on till noon.

Then we slept in the afternoon and started work again in the evening. At midday it was too hot to do anything. An unrelenting sun glared out of a slate-blue sky; with no hint of a breeze the heat became suffocating. It seemed to overcome every living thing on the face of the earth. The vegetables in the kitchen garden, the grass, even the hostile swards of the stinging nettles bowed over in defeat. By early afternoon our three baby calves, which normally had only milk, needed an extra drink of water from a lemonade bottle fitted with a large rubber teat.

Tom abandoned any idea of show jumping. He could not risk injuring the horses permanently by the constant jarring they suffered on landing on hard ground. We stopped working them, turned them out in the field during the night but brought them in during the day to give them some peace from the flies.

At first we enjoyed the sunshine and took pride in our suntans. But after a few days the torrid heat became unbearable at midday. Even in the evening ordinary household chores like cooking and ironing made most women feel like candidates for martyrdom. Not that anyone felt like eating big meals – like most people we were living on a diet of salads, sandwiches, ice-cream and Coke. Britain's drinking habits were changing too: beer drinkers were developing a distinct preference for iced lager instead of blood-heat flat bitter. Hereford's local cider factory, using apples from the orchards all around us, saw sales rocket. It estimated that every extra hour of sunshine meant an extra thousand gallons of cider sold.

The weather got hotter and hotter. June 25 was the hottest June day in Britain for twenty-eight years. At Wimbledon the centre-court players were sweltering in temperatures over 100 degrees. The next day the temperature in London reached 95 degrees – the highest ever recorded there. Our friends described the city as a fetid swamp lying in a haze of pollution. At the weekends the roads were packed with traffic, as people tried to get out of the cities. Long queues built up on the routes to the

West Country and Wales. Many jams were caused by cars conking out with boiling radiators.

On our own farm, water for the stock remained a central and unremitting problem. We had turned the cattle onto the hay-field to clear up the grass on the headland. There they were drinking from the trough supplied by our only remaining reserves, the well with the hand pump. Every day we made four visits to the trough, pumping about ten troughfuls for them altogether. By the end of a week we all had over-developed biceps and a total antipathy to pumping.

To this was now added a new hazard – insects. The cattle were being tormented by a plague of gadflies. These are harmless-looking insects, striped like a small wasp, that hover. Cattle notice this hovering action and 'gad' about or, more accurately, go plain berserk. They tear around like maniacs with their tails stuck straight in the air and a characteristic tense gait. Angel, our house-cow, normally a very earthbound bovine, had been known to jump a three-foot wire fence when being pursued by a gadfly.

The cattle's reaction to these insects is hardly surprising in view of the gadfly's highly unpleasant way of life. The flies lay their eggs on the hairs on the legs and underside of cattle. After hatching out the larvae eat into the animal, going right through them until they arrive under the skin on the back the following spring. They grow there forming quite large lumps and finally emerge from a hole they bore, fall to the ground to form a pupa from which the adult insects hatch to start the whole vile cycle again. There are no insect repellents to protect the cattle, although most farmers now use a wash in the spring or autumn that is absorbed by the bloodstream and kills the developing larvae.

To enable our cattle to escape from the gadflies we had to let them into one of the sheds in the barn during the day. And there they happily guzzled our precious domestic water supply from the automatic drinking fountains. We could not tie up the bowls as we had done in the winter because the cattle desperately needed water during those scorching days.

It was not only the year of the gadfly. The whole insect world was on the move. The air seemed full of them. At times we would not have been at all surprised to see a cloud of locusts swarming over the horizon.

Aphids settled like spots of green mould on our bare arms as we walked about. Plants in the garden were covered with them. The pink Dorothy Perkins rose which had once smothered the front porch was a sorry sight: delicate pink blooms bleached a blowsy white, blighted with mildew, and the whole plant from root to tip was covered with greenfly. The pretty heads of the columbine drooped under the weight of the same fly, whilst even the hardy stinging nettles had a green scaly mantle. In the fields around us corn crops were being decimated by the minute green devils.

At night we had the choice of the heat or being covered in insects. Great black forest beetles, swarms of flies, and moths and midges of assorted shapes and sizes zoomed into the house and gyrated a dance of death around the light bulbs. If the windows were closed we could hear them tap-tapping against the panes beating themselves insensible.

By the end of June our worst fears about the water shortage were realized. The pond dried up. All that was left of it was a basin of cracked earth with a soft centre of oozy grey mud. It looked uncannily like a shot from the sixties film, 'The Day the Earth Caught Fire'.

And according to the weathermen there was more hot weather to come – years and years of it. The World Meteorological Office issued a report concluding there would be more hot summers. Pollution was building up above the earth, producing a green-house effect that was heating up the whole globe.

9. July 1976 (I)

At first the heat-wave had its agreeable moments. Perhaps it is memories of sodden summer holidays in childhood, washed-out Wimbledons and wet Whitsuns that invariably make a hot spell seem a welcome bonus to the summer. There is a traditional picture of the green English countryside basking in the summer sunshine that adorns many a tourist poster and chocolate box. It still exists in places like Herefordshire: the villages of black and white cottages, the lush pastures and hedgerows with fat cattle lazing in the shade of majestic oak trees. Before the sun scorched the countryside to death it enhanced its beauty, giving us throughout the day a sequence of views of breathtaking beauty.

At the beginning of July the early mornings, in particular, were unexpectedly peaceful and enchanting. In the still air the dawn chorus was sweet and clear while the farmyard and fields beyond were bathed in a gentle light from a benign sun in a sapphire sky.

But this idyll was abruptly shattered at about seven o'clock. There would be an outburst of bellowing and mooing, stamping and clattering accompanied by a chorus of wild yapping and barking from the dogs. Round in the stackyard the cattle would be all over the place, blundering about among the bales of hay and straw in search of some protective shade

We had moved the stock onto fresh pasture, the twelve-acre field hip-high with grass that lay behind the stackyard. Normally the wide spreading oaks and beeches flanking it would have provided plenty of shade, and protection from the gadflies. But not that July. We had to herd the cattle into the barn every day as soon as the wretched flies went into action. We waited until the attack began, for to move the stock a moment sooner would have given them even more time to get at our precious supply of water for the house

I used to try and keep an eye on the cattle as I went about my morning chores – milking the cow, feeding the chickens and seeing to the baby calves which were fostered on the cow to drink her surplus milk. But all too often I would miss the first signs of restlessness. Then there would be a stampede out of the field and into the stackyard.

By ten o'clock the heat was really on – often the thermometer was hovering about the 90-degree mark. By lunchtime the sweltering atmosphere was almost intolerable. It was so totally unlike Britain; the air seemed completely lifeless. There was no breeze, nothing stirred, grass plants and trees drooped in defeat. We wondered if anything would survive it for long.

Even in the evenings there was no respite from the heat. It was as if the ground had become so hot during the day that it radiated heat long after the sun went down. Only in the still hours before dawn was there a refreshing coolness in the air. Tom and I particularly missed our normal evening walks round the farm. The days seemed long gone when we had strolled in the lingering summer dusk checking the stock, fences and water troughs and discussing plans for the future.

The heat affected everyone and everything. The house was plagued by flies which seemed quite undaunted by the strings of fly-killing strips decorating the kitchen. I was reluctant to gas the lot with an aerosol because the baby was at the vacuum-cleaning stage. Every piece of straw and scrap of fluff on the floor went straight into his mouth. Meals were like a magician's turn with food thrown onto the table and then whipped off again, before the flies could get busy.

Wood warped and metal joints loosened as the temperatures went on soaring. We still had a drop of water left in the well but the pump on it caused endless trouble because the joints in the pipes had expanded and let in air. Gates and wooden fencing collapsed with heat exhaustion. To make matters worse, when we first went to mend them the heads of the hammers flew off. From then on tools with wooden handles were kept in a bucket of water.

The backs of the kitchen chairs rattled and the bars of the baby's playpen became so loose that one day he made a bid for freedom and got his head stuck between them. It was not long before our tempers became as warped as the wood

The first of July marked the start of our water buying and begging activities. We decided we could not risk any longer trying to get by on our own resources. We would have to look further afield for water. The pond had dried up completely. All the rain-water tanks were empty. I rang the Water Authority and asked for a tankerful. Other people were obviously in the same predicament because it took us over half an hour to get through to the Water Board – all the telephone lines were busy from 8.30 a.m. The authority officials were helpful, and promised a load that afternoon.

Our first sight of the tanker rather stunned us. We had no idea of the quantity of water our cattle drank until we saw the tank sitting there on the back of a flatbed lorry. It was a great gleaming vehicle, remarkably clean after its trip up our dusty drive. The cylindrical tank looked enormous. It proved however to contain only 1000 gallons of water which barely half-filled our cisterns.

The whole operation was remarkably like a fire-fighting exercise. The driver backed up to the barn, leapt out of his cab and unrolled a long canvas hose-pipe. With this he scaled the ladder to the cisterns in the loft, shoved the end at Tom and disappeared back to the lorry. There was a sound of revving up and the water started to gush into the tanks. It shot out under great pressure and we had to struggle to keep the hose-pipe in the right direction. After months of seeing that precious commodity dribble out of almost empty taps we could hardly believe our eyes – there was so much of it all at once. But within a few minutes the tanks were half-full and the tanker was empty.

The driver rolled up the hose-pipe and emptied the dregs into a bucket. 'No sense wasting any. Not when you're paying the price you are,' he remarked cheerfully. We offered him a cup of tea.

'No thanks. You pay mainly on distance and time. It would cost you a fortune, mate. Besides I've another three loads to deliver this morning. Lots of people are out of water, I'm delivering all over the county.'

The tanker's load did not last us long. In three days the cattle and the house had accounted for the lot. However often we filled the trough in the field the cattle seemed permanently short of water. As we stood watching them gulp great draughts of the precious liquid, their thirst seemed inexhaustible. In fact, I worked out that each animal was drinking between ten and twelve gallons a day. On a normal spring day about five gallons was all they needed, while when the grass was lush and wet they would drink as little as a gallon a day each. Human beings use a gallon a day on cooking and drinking.

It was obvious we could not continue to buy water for the stock by the tanker-load because it was just too expensive. The price for the 1000 gallons was almost £10. People on the mains receiving water through metered pipes paid only 56p for the same quantity. Tom decided the only solution was to devise our own tanker. We could stop using the stock lorry as a horse-box and convert it into a water carrier by loading five of the largest rainwater tanks onto it. It meant, however, we would have to make public our predicament. So far we had kept the calamity of the pond dark, telling our neighbours airily that it still had 'a drop in it'.

At first we considered drawing water from the stream in Micklebury but then decided to confide in John Hopkins, our nearest neighbour as the crow flies. His farmyard was easily accessible and large enough for us to manoeuvre the lorry – both crucial requirements but hard to come by in an area of old-fashioned small holdings.

John readily offered us as much water as we wanted. Unfortunately the pressure on his supply was so low that it took five hours to fill the tanks on the first trip. This did not daunt John. An ingenious farmer, if ever there was one, he thought up several other ways to help us.

He knew only too well what it was like to live without running water. For eighteen months he had drawn water daily for his stock, until he could afford a mains connection. His solution to the problem had been simple, if highly unorthodox. He bought a trailer tanker which could be pulled behind a tractor, and tooled up a stand-pipe to fit a nearby fire hydrant. The pressure from the hydrant was so great it filled the tanker in only five minutes. He had since lost the stand-pipe, so he and Tom spent an afternoon examining all the hydrants in the area to see if the fire brigade had left one behind. Their activities did not go unnoticed: suspicious onlookers peeped out from behind cottage curtains. At one place a man rushed out of his house and demanded to know what they were doing.

'That's all right,' he said when they explained, 'I don't care. I don't give a damn what you're doing so long as you don't interfere with my water supply.'

Then John had another brainwave. He had planned for some time to install a water trough in a field of his close to the main pipe that went through to Micklebury. Tapping the main at that point would mean the pressure was much greater than higher up at his farm. He got permission from the Water Authority, and he and Tom dug down and attached a plastic pipe to the farm pipe-line just after it branched off the main.

This became our chief water-point – indeed our lifeline. Tom now started almost daily journeys to it. The new connection saved about four hours in the filling. Even so the whole job still took a good three hours by the time Tom had driven the lorry down the road, filled the tanks, driven back and then pumped the water into the drinking trough. It was time we could ill-afford to spare during the busy summer days, an exasperating extra burden. Often we did not get to bed until after midnight.

At first the village was agog. What was that lorry doing going up and down that road every day? Don Parker, in particular, could hardly contain his curiosity. By coincidence or by design he worked in his orchard in the evenings and watched, his face dark with bewilderment, as Tom passed on both his outward and return journeys. Finally Don just happened to be crossing the road with his herd of cows as Tom chugged along with a lorry-load of water and was forced to stop.

'What you on then?' Don asked.

Tom took pity on him. 'I suppose if I don't tell you, you'll lie awake all night worrying yourself to death. I'm carting water from the main down by the road which leads to the Hopkinses' farm.'

'Arrh,' Don said with relief. His face cleared as a further mystery was solved. 'So that's what the scuffling is in the road down by the bend.' They missed nothing in Micklebury

Indeed Tom's water-carting became something of an institution in the village. At first he spent the hour waiting for the tanks to fill sitting on the tail-board feeling bored. But a couple living in a cottage nearby started to invite him in for a cup of coffee. They became our firm friends.

The Hopkinses, too, often made an occasion of Tom's visits.

Though they could not see the lorry from their farmhouse they always knew soon enough when Tom was there. His activities meant their own cold water was cut off. So John or Sue would often come down for a talk, or ask Tom up to the farm. Many other people stopped and chatted. Having a gossip at our water-point became a village custom. Joady was a frequent passer-by. He would sit on the bank beside Tom for a few minutes and then say triumphantly, 'Still on this job then? Still carting water, eh?' He was the possessor of an eighty-foot well which was still giving water, and was entitled to relish his good fortune.

The water helped supplement our domestic supplies as well as water the stock. We used it mainly for washing. It was too precious to spend on things like flushing the lavatory more often. On many an evening Morag or I knelt on the tail-board of the lorry washing our hair in a rubber yard bucket. It was more refreshing than iced lager after a long dusty day.

In the first half of July we had a renewed burst of hope. There were signs that the heat-wave might be just a 'hot spell' and not the first phase of a Mediterranean summer. On the evening of 3 July, for instance, the eternally blue sky grew black and overcast, the air still and humid. The storm, to our immense disappointment, went round us but returned for ten minutes during the night. We awoke to a world that was fresh and bright, washed clean of the suffocating dust that had shrouded it.

That evening the thunder clouds built up again. We watched, with mounting excitement, as the sky grew dark and heavy. It was as though it had been dry for so long that only an enormous celestial force could make the clouds release the rain. Even the swallows were still flying high in the belief that it would never come.

Then it started; a few heavy drops to begin with, and then hesitantly, a little more. Suddenly the storm seemed to overcome the resistance, and rain bucketed down. All the rain we had missed in the past month seemed to come at once.

We rushed out to the lorry and pulled and heaved at the heavy rainwater tanks. At last we got them unloaded and dragged them into their former places under the guttering pipes from which the water was cascading onto the ground. In less than half an hour the tanks were overflowing and we were drenched to the skin.

There were several moments that July when our fatalism about the weather gave way to wild optimism. One such moment was after that first thunderstorm. With the water streaming down our faces and squelching in our shoes life looked good again. In the Midlands the scorching summer of the previous year had been punctuated in this way, by regular thunderstorms, which made for a damp July. It looked after that thunderstorm as though the weather might now follow the same pattern.

We were wrong. The thunderstorm was an exception. The trials and tribulations of the summer had hardly begun.

All over southern Britain crops were starting to fail in the relentless glare of the sun. Farmers were losing the battle with the heat; many feared massively reduced profits; some even bankruptcy. Strawberry growers had already seen their crops wilt in the sunshine as the season lasted a mere ten days instead of six weeks. Other fruit farmers faced an equally lean time. Currants, raspberries and gooseberries were ripening so fast they could not be picked in time.

But the main fear was for winter vegetables. In many parts of the country market gardeners were struggling to raise crops in dust-bowl conditions. Kale was said to be 'very rough', sugar beet in East Anglia had germinated poorly, sprouts in Lincolnshire were dying – there were forecasts of 3p a sprout by the winter, and the Devon swedes were going to be small and hard. There were also likely to be shortages of carrots, cauliflowers, cabbages, celery and parsnips.

Because of the lack of rain, grain was beginning to ripen without first swelling up. Combine harvesters had been in action since the end of June, at least a week earlier than ever recorded before.

Our own vegetable garden, so crucial to the economy of our household, was in no better shape than the nation's market gardens. Reports of impending vegetable shortages spurred me into action with the watering-can. We used the washing-up water regularly now for this purpose, one more chore in a day already crammed with them.

It was something I was loath to do because it seems that once you start watering plants you have to keep on, and it becomes an almost full-time job. Without artificial watering the weaker plants may die but the stronger ones put down long roots to the water deep in the soil. This theory worked well until the temperature reached the nineties, and the heat shrivelled everything in sight.

So we began to recycle our meagre water supply yet again, baling the washing-up water into buckets and pouring it on the garden. It was so hot that after several weeks the sun's rays made the plastic watering-can disintegrate.

My efforts with the washing-up water were just drops in the desert. It kept the plants alive but the scorching heat stunted their growth. Lettuces put out about six little leaves and then bolted, the broad beans gave up half-way through the crop with the upper pods black and empty. The french beans made a valiant effort but the pods swelled up in a day and became tough and inedible.

Fire was a further hazard the heat-wave brought to the countryside. The National Farmers' Union appealed to the public to regard the countryside as a tinderbox that could explode into widespread devastation at the touch of a match or of a burning cigarette.

We did not have to look far to see what happened when people ignored that warning. Tom helped to put out two blazes in one day. The first was in a hedgerow just outside Micklebury, clearly started by a cigarette end from a passing car. The other was in the local market where another cigarette had ignited a pile of rubbish. Two days later a huge forest fire raged at Presteigne, only a few miles away. Soon there was mile upon mile of burnt roadside hedgerows. Friends who had driven through East Anglia told us of hundreds of acres of corn reduced to ash there.

Early in July the Government woke up to the fact that Britain was in for a water shortage. It decided that powers must be taken to restrict not just the use of water in and around homes, but in factories, processing plants, and the host of other commercial and industrial operations which are, in a modern society, the huge consumers of water. The water authorities already had powers to apply for 'drought orders' to restrict the use of hose-pipes for car washing and garden watering. Now they could apply for power to stop all non-essential uses like the cleaning of buildings, watering of parks, golf courses and sports grounds, commercial car washing, and the filling of swimming pools.

But the Government still held back from the most drastic step of all – rationing of mains water to private homes. They saw no likelihood of this being necessary before the end of August. Mr John Silkin, the Minister of Planning and Local Government, who was overlord of the water authorities, went out of his way to reassure us of this. At Peterborough on 5 July he stated: 'Precautions will affect only the worst-hit areas.' He went on to say, 'There will be special consideration for agriculture, industry, food processing, old people and essential services. It will not become a case of people being without the necessary amount of water to carry on their normal lives.'

What the Government did not stress was that rationing for home use had already begun in Somerset and south-west Wales. Water supplies there were cut off to many homes at night. Yet I suppose Mr Silkin was right in a way. For life with little or no water had become for thousands of us by now the normal pattern.

Indeed at much the same time as Mr Silkin was making his speech, I was frantically telephoning the Water Authority. The tanker-load of water we had expected the day before had failed to appear. We were managing to get enough water for the cattle by carting it from the Hopkinses'. But by the time the water arrived at the farm it was too dirty for human consumption. Our improvised water wagon was far from hygienic. The tanks on the lorry were, after all, normally stationed under the rainwater pipes from the farm buildings. The sides and bases were coated with green slime and they were too heavy and too closely packed into the lorry to clean out on arrival at the Hopkinses'. We had no proper lids and, to prevent half the water slopping over the tops on the bumpy ride up the drive to the farm, we had a collection of old doors, polythene sheets and tarpaulins to tie over them.

These tended to fall on the floor of the lorry or onto the road when they were removed and picked up grit, straw and general muck. However desperate we were for water for our domestic needs it seemed too risky to introduce this unwholesome liquid into our quirky plumbing system. We just had to have one tanker of clean drinkable water every ten days or so.

'I'm sorry, but all private deliveries have been stopped,' said the voice at the other end of the line when I rang the Water Authority. 'We need all our tankers to ferry supplies to people where the mains have failed. If it was up to me I would let you have some, but the order comes from higher up. I've four other people expecting water this morning and I hate to let them down. I don't know what you can do.'

It was the first indication in our area that the mains supply was now in trouble. The Herefordshire mains system drew its water from many sources, from a complex patchwork of bore-holes, springs, rivers and service reservoirs. These sources, like our own wells, were now drying up. The authority countered by setting up tanks in the affected villages, tanks which were filled from a fleet of tankers, some hired from as far away as London. From these local water points the villagers could draw water by the bucketful. By the end of August there were 300 tanks installed in different parts of the Herefordshire countryside. Long before stand-pipes were introduced, with much publicity, into Devon, villagers in Herefordshire were drawing their water in buckets and jugs from a local tank, as if they were Bedouin in the Middle East drawing their water from the nearest well.

Stand-pipes also began to make an appearance in the county. One of the first was in the scattered community at Orleton Common and the Goggin. The villagers there had been waiting eighteen years for a mains supply, and they took it very hard when they were asked to pay a £5 deposit for a key to use an emergency stand-pipe. All except one family refused. The majority solved the problem in their own way. They broke the pipe lock, and helped themselves.

By moving their tankers over to the task of coping with the problems of those whose mains had run dry, the Water Authority had left those of us on private supplies literally high and dry. Whatever the Government may have said about priority for agriculture, and about fair shares for all, the authority had clearly decided that priority must go to maintaining some sort of supply to users connected to the mains. Yet these mains users did not have to pay anything extra for their emergency supplies. It was clear, too, that this was no short-term problem.

Not that we were completely ignored. The authority said if it was practical to supply unconnected properties by tanker it would be glad to do so. Unfortunately it was often not practical.

As an alternative the authority was prepared to make arrangements for stand-pipe supplies where 'the availability of manpower and the water itself makes this feasible'. And there was the cost. As the authority put it, 'Supplies by tanker or stand-pipe to unconnected properties have to be charged for at cost which can, of, course, be significant.'

It undertook, too, that a bank of water would be maintained at

the Broomy Hill treatment plant in Hereford for use by privately
hauled tankers.

Nearer home our neighbour, Rivers, who had been receiving
two tanker-loads a week, was in a state of permanent anxiety. His
brother, the owner of a milking herd, was in a similar predicament
and was faced with the prospect of selling up. Like us they were
finding it physically impossible to cart all the water their stock
needed, especially as the hot weather doubled the cattle's thirst.

A few days later the Welsh National Water Development
Authority and the neighbouring Severn–Trent Authority announced there was a serious deficit of water in a long list of places
including Gloucester, Cheltenham, Tewkesbury, Radnor, the
Cotswolds, the Teme Valley. Malvern, with its famous mineral
water, was also on the list.

But we had, at long last, an ally. The Leominster District
Council weighed in to try and obtain supplies for unconnected
villages and hamlets. It announced it was to invoke the 1973
Water Resources Act in an effort to improve supplies to parts of
north Herefordshire including Micklebury. Under the Act,
claimed the council, the authority had a duty to supply 'whole-
some water for domestic purposes'. Where it was not practicable
to supply it by pipe, it must be supplied some other way at
'reasonable' cost.

For the first time we realized the Water Authority was not
doing us a favour by delivering us water by tanker. Apparently
it had a legal duty to do so. But still no tanker was forthcoming.
On the Friday we faced a weekend without any water for the
house. Tom was up until two o'clock in the morning hauling
water for the stock and it was impossible to find time for an extra
journey to supply the house. We had to have a tanker.

In desperation I rang the local council's health department.

'It's going to take an outbreak of typhoid before people realize
how terrible this situation is,' I fumed. 'I'm on a filthy farm, I've
a thirteen-month-old baby and there are three adults in the house.
None of us has had a bath for a fortnight and our nearest water
supply is a mile away. Can't someone in this welfare state, which
hands out colour television sets at the drop of a hat, help us? We
don't object to the enormous price but even then we can't get the
most essential amenity of life.'

I had prepared myself for the health inspector giving me the

D

usual line: 'There's a drought, you know. Other people are without water and everything possible is being done.' Instead he was sympathetic and helpful. There wasn't a lot they could do, he explained. They could inform the water people but they could not force them to do anything about it. He would phone the authority and see what he could do.

Later that afternoon a tanker arrived.

10. July 1976 (II)

There was a timelessness about the hot dusty days of that July. Life seemed to come to a standstill in a world bounded by an endless blue sky above a dying landscape. Time and date were irrelevant. Noon seemed to stretch from ten o'clock in the morning until four in the afternoon. Apart from the breeding cycle of our friends, the swallows, there were few seasonal milestones. We were surrounded by an unchanging view of yellow prematurely ripened corn, dying grass and drooping leaves.

By the middle of the month the heat had transformed our pasture into a dusty savanna. The dry grass crunched under our feet like potato crisps. Baked and bleached by the sun the pastures looked more like fields of stubble. Only a few green spikes of thistles and docks survived to remind us of their former green richness.

On the other side of the drive, in the field with the five pines, the turf had been burnt bare in patches where the soil was thin over the rock. Unmolested by cattle for five weeks, in any other year it would have been a sea of foot-high grass.

The four-acre pasture we had hoped to mow for hay at the end of July was little better. From a distance it looked fairly green, but closer inspection revealed a forest of spikes unadorned by foliage. All the grass we had on the farm was in the field around the former dew-pond. We had the cattle there now. But even that grass had been flattened by heat and hooves, so the field looked like tired heathland after an August Bank Holiday.

Some of our neighbours had no grass at all and were being forced to feed hay to their stock. After a lot of heart-searching we decided there was nothing for it but to start selling some of the cattle. A few more dry weeks and we would have nothing fit to sell.

We booked the eight largest animals into the market a few days later. Some were old friends; Rosie, the red heifer who drank our water at night in the winter; The Murderess, so named because as a calf she would shove her head into the milk bucket, clamp her teeth on the finger proffered for her to suck and charge at the wall. The idea seemed to be to amputate your finger and crush your hand all in one quick operation. Then there was Big William a red and white steer with the gentle disposition of the truly obese, and Red Micky who would wait by the door at feeding time and streak out of the shed, escaping into the open as the luckless feeder was trying to avoid being trampled underfoot as the other cattle surged towards the manger.

There was no hope of replacing these cattle with young calves that would not need to be turned out to grass for many months. For we had to cope not only with the weather that July, but also with the imbalance in agriculture caused by Britain's peculiar position in the Common Market. Sometimes we felt we were trying to earn a living with both hands tied behind our backs.

When prices were low in 1974 the fall of the market had been exacerbated by cheap European meat being dumped in Britain because of high Common Market export subsidies. Now the trade was going the other way. The Italians and Germans were buying thousands of British calves. As their farming costs, except labour, were only 10 per cent above ours while their returns were almost twice as high, they could afford to pay exorbitant prices. Despite this, many British farmers were still buying calves enthusiastically. They believed the old adage about the bidder against them: 'If it's worth that to him, it's worth that to me.' We were not prepared to do this. With the Government's commitment to a cheap food policy we could not see any way that a week-old calf could be worth £60 to us. Yet even if we could not afford to replace our stock immediately we would have to sell some.

By the time we took our cattle to market scores of farmers were running out of grass and water. The market was full of sheep, many desperately thin after a month of poor grazing. In one pen an emaciated ewe lay panting beside a dead lamb she had just produced. Prices were equally slender; a third down on the previous month. I saw Tom talking to an acquaintance, a small fair woman with a face lined with weary despair.

He told me later she farmed up in the hills on the Welsh border. 'It's sheer hell up there. No grass, no water. They can't even get tankers up to the farms. People are selling whole flocks for slaughter.'

Surprisingly, however, people still wanted to buy cattle. Trade on the smaller animals had 'eased', as they say in the auctioneering business. Dropped like a stone is more an accurate description. One bunch of the lighter five hundredweight heifers made only £20 a hundredweight. But luckily for us the demand for bigger cattle had picked up on the previous week. It was one of those odd days when the sellers had stayed away fearing a further drop in prices, but the buyers had flocked in hoping for bargains.

Our cattle fetched a good price, well up to our expectations. We were only just in time: because of the drought the market did not return to that level for the rest of the summer.

In the crowds on the wooden benches in the amphitheatre of the auction ring sat Joady's nephew. He was studiously noting down the prices. By evening the whole village would know what our cattle made and probably our return per acre, gross profit and net income as well. Working out your neighbours' profits, or their losses, is a popular pastime in farming areas – and all the more fun if you have only a few clues to go on. We drove home knowing that if cattle prices went on falling – and they did – we would have no choice but to slog on until the autumn.

Near the middle of July came the next brief break in the heat-wave. One morning we woke to an overcast sky and the sound of distant rumbling. At first we thought it must be blasting at the local quarry. But it was thunder. Away to the west we could see a storm tipping rain down on the Welsh mountains. On the radio the programmes were interrupted with traffic warnings about torrential rain and flooding on the M6 in the Midlands. At nine o'clock in the morning the first drops fell on our farm. And after three minutes it stopped. We were crushed with disappointment.

But later that day, as I was washing-up after supper, I heard a swishing sound outside. Then we realized it was really raining. There followed another mad scramble to get the tanks off the lorry and under the guttering pipes. In the pink-tinged sky there was only a narrow belt of clouds but they were heading straight for us. 'That rain's for us,' I shouted jubilantly above the storm. And so it was. It rained heavily for an hour, stopped, and then rained for another half hour. We were lucky. All Micklebury got was one short shower.

Our irrepressible optimism returned. For the next few days the sun disappeared in a heavy grey sky. The wind was in the west bringing the sound of traffic and trains and the hope of more rain. We laughed with other waterless friends about the reactions we all had when it rained. For everyone, storms now prompted a frenzy of activity. We all rushed outside and bathed, washed our hair and clothes.

Showers and drizzle went on until St Swithin's day, 15 July, which dawned auspiciously damp and overcast. There were a few light showers in the morning followed by a downpour in the evening for good measure. According to legend if it rains on St Swithin's day it will rain for the next forty days. But the newspapers were quick to point out that in practice the weather had never fulfilled the saint's predictions. 'Normal rainfall and normal temperatures' was the more prosaic forecast for the next thirty days from the meteorological office.

An American writer was predicting another Ice Age. He managed to fit the summers of 1975 and 1976 into his hypothesis by claiming the intergalactical age was breaking up so we could expect extremes of temperature, both hot and cold, before the ice spread inevitably from the north.

With a neat sense of timing the Government picked the following day to introduce its Drought Bill. It announced that if supplies were rationed agriculture would be given top priority. This buttressed our optimism further. We noted from the papers that on the Continent the French government and the Common Market Commission were taking more positive measures to help farmers. In the great beef- and corn-growing areas of central and northern France no measurable rainfall had fallen for four months.

Worst affected were the grass, hay and maize crops in Brittany and Normandy. The French government feared the reduction in agricultural exports – France is the Common Market's main food producer – could seriously affect its balance of payments.

We watched, horrified, as a television news report showed French milking herds being sold for slaughter as the grass ran out. But matters, it seemed, were worse than that. On the way to market one Wednesday Tom gave a lift to four French students from Brittany. They told him cattle were dying of thirst on farms in their home area because the slaughter-houses were full. A friend in France wrote: 'I have used the air-conditioning in the car every day since the middle of May. It is so hot we have not had a good night's sleep since then. Thousands of peasant farmers face bankruptcy and the situation is tense because the farmers are a much more powerful political force than in Britain. Even people like us who have a stream running through the garden dare not water the lawn. Any patch of green is likely to receive a Molotov cocktail from an irate French countryman.'

Fodder was so short in France that hay was fetching £100 a ton compared with £30 a ton in Britain. Despite high freight charges some farmers were finding it worthwhile to import hay from us.

The French government announced a number of measures to help the stricken areas, including a ban on the export of fodder. The army was sent in to operate a 'straw lift' from the south to the worst-affected areas.

In other countries things were almost as bad. In vast areas of northern Italy no rain had fallen for eighty-five days and more than a million head of cattle faced premature slaughter. The Italian government was investigating the possibility of importing water from Austria and Switzerland. Even in Switzerland some areas were in the grip of the drought and the government there was also trying to prevent the wholesale slaughter of cattle.

The Common Market Commission announced an emergency scheme to help dairy farmers.

It enabled cows to be sold more readily for beef by allowing them to be sold into intervention – stocks in cold store – at a guaranteed price.

All this was depressing news for us. It was partly the Continental demand for British beef that had kept the market buoyant. Now prices were falling steadily as housewives replaced the traditional Sunday roast with salads in the hot weather. At the same time supply was increasing as farmers sold off their cattle as soon as they were ready to slaughter.

In Britain the break in the drought was short-lived. St Swithin's prediction and the meteorological office's forecast were proved to be totally wrong within forty-eight hours. The temperature rose into the upper eighties again, the cattle returned to the barn during the day, and our water was desperately short once more. We turned off the water in the barn to conserve supplies for the house, but it meant in turn that we had no cold water during the day. The lavatory began to emit an odour reminiscent of a cheap Spanish hotel even after half a bottle of bleach had been emptied down it. The flies were worse than ever and I had no choice but to start a campaign of mass extermination with an aerosol. This worked for a short while, but hundreds more settled on the outside of the back door waiting to come in as soon as it was opened.

More villages in the county went dry as demand for water exceeded supply and the pressure in the mains dropped. In an extraordinary statement, the Water Authority blamed 'water-hogs' for the shortages. It attacked people in the valleys for wasting water by watering their lawns and washing their cars, so there was none left for people living on higher ground. Few farmers accepted that explanation. People in general do not wash their cars during the day, except at weekends, because they are at work. Nor do they water their lawns in the heat of the day because it would kill the grass off even faster.

A far more plausible reason was simply that people used more water during the heat-wave for drinking and washing. And, of course, there was the greater thirst of the farm animals. These outnumber people in Herefordshire and they were all drinking at least twice as much as normal. And as brooks and pools dried up, farmers with a mains supply started to give their stock water from the tap.

When the next tanker arrived the driver was contemptuous of the official explanations. 'You know and I know. The public aren't fools. It's all lies, I don't know why the authority doesn't come clean. It is a simple matter of demand exceeding supply.' He was not usually despondent. His normal mood was cheerful, and he had inscribed on the dust of his cab the words: 'As seen on ATV', because it had been featured in a television report.

As the heat-wave entered its second month there were some strange developments in wildlife around the farm. Small rodents were obviously having a hard time finding water. On many mornings we found a dead rat or mouse in the bucket of water left out for the dogs. The dogs themselves seemed almost unaffected by the hot weather, apart from needing more water than usual. But they, after all, had less to do than any of us. The alsatian's main job was to bark furiously when strangers approached the farm. Maggie and Risky, the Jack Russell terriers, took a break from rat-catching and spent the summer snoozing in shady corners. Even our two collies had only a ten-minute stint morning and evening rushing about to collect the cattle.

But it was certainly the year of the insect, and above all of the ladybird. These tiny spotted creatures, which in an ordinary year never attracted more than an occasional glance as they went about their business in the fields or the garden, suddenly seemed to be everywhere, within doors as well as without. On beaches all along the West Country coastline people complained that they were being attacked by swarms of ladybirds. A learned discussion began in the correspondence columns of the papers as to whether they really did bite, or whether they were just clutching with their tiny feet as they tried to get moisture from the damp and sweaty bodies of sunbathers.

It was a problem which, like that of the foxes, went back to the mild winter. This had allowed exceptionally large numbers of hibernating ladybirds to survive until the spring. Weather conditions in the spring in turn favoured a build-up of aphids, which are the natural food of ladybirds. This led to a further upsurge in the ladybird population. Then came the drought, which meant that the plants on which the aphids fed ripened swiftly and matured early – leaving the aphids without their food, and the ladybirds without their aphids. Driven desperate, the ladybirds swarmed off in search of nourishment anywhere they might find it, even on the bodies of the dozing crowds on the beaches. But their search was largely in vain, and by the autumn the scientists were to warn us that ladybirds had perished in very large numbers.

The drought certainly suited the butterflies. At noon the kitchen garden was decorated with dancing Cabbage Whites intent on producing a horde of offspring to decimate what was left of our autumn cabbages and cauliflowers. The more uncommon butterflies were also there in increasing numbers. As early as April we had been struck by the prevalence of Tortoise-Shells. They brought colour to the garden which was sadly lacking in flowers. There were reports in the papers of sightings of rare species. A letter to *The Times* claimed that a Camberwell Beauty had been spotted at Shoreham in Kent. The naturalists explained that the less commonly sighted butterflies are in fact with us in a normal summer, but tended to gravitate to the high life in the tree-tops. Lack of moisture was bringing them down to human-eye level in their search for water.

The quest for water nearly brought several animals literally to a sticky end in the muddy remains of the dew-pond. We checked our stock daily, making a regular pilgrimage to see if any strays were trapped in the grave of the pond. A neighbour's ewe and lamb, which had decided that the grass was greener on our side of the fence, were the first casualties. Morag spotted them early one morning, when she noticed that what had appeared to be a lump of wood on the surface of the mud had suddenly moved. But now the lump turned out to be the ewe. A smaller log nearby was her lamb. Both were close to death, as they had been stuck fast for at least three days.

Using ropes and planks we rescued the lamb without much difficulty. After a few shaky steps he bounded round the edge of the pond baa-ing blue murder for his mother. Freeing the ewe was a much more difficult job. She made no effort to struggle, so we were dealing with dead weight. Eventually we dragged her out and she lay like a beached whale on the cracked mud. When our neighbour collected her she was still alive, but she died later on that afternoon.

Another animal trapped was one of our show jumpers, a big chestnut thoroughbred called Fred. He was tempted to take a cooling mud bath one evening, rolled in the dew-pond and got stuck fast. He managed to get out on his own just as we rushed over the field with the rescue gear. But in the process he struck one leg with a flying hoof. The injury put him out of action for the rest of the summer.

After these incidents it seemed a wise idea to have the pond cleared. And if it ever rained again a cleared pond would hold more water. Sid Williams, the contractor who had severed our telephone cable back in the autumn, came up to do the job.

Most of the time he was a ditching and drainage man. Now he was overwhelmed with urgent requests to clear dried-up pools and to dig new water-holes. But he owed us a favour, so he came up on a Sunday. Sid had his own stories about the drought even though the theme was becoming all too familiar. Where he lived there were three wells on a slope that had formerly supplied two farms and a row of five cottages. They had been dry for the past six months and one of the farmers affected had been forced to sell half his cattle at a loss of £15 a head.

It took him only a day to clear the pond and by the time he had finished it was three times its original size. The sludge came off the bottom like icing off a Christmas cake. In the process he unearthed some drains leading out of the pond – a sign of another age when they had been needed to take away surplus water.

The weekly weather forecast promised us rain – showers in the early part of the week and then again towards the weekend. It was wrong again.

Towards the end of July we began to feel as trapped as the animals who had strayed into the dew-pond. We still faced the dreary daily task of carting water for the stock. A month had passed since the pond had dried up, but we faced another eight weeks before we could think of selling the cattle or hope for enough rain to improve our water supplies. And it was clear the Government was intending to do nothing special to help farmers without water.

As far as the eye could see the landscape was parched and bare. In the woodland surrounding the farm the oaks and beeches were turning brown from lack of water. Younger saplings were dying by the hundreds.

Only one plantation was thriving. This was a newly planted patch of conifers bordering on our farm. A marshy wilderness of gorse, ferns and particularly tenacious brambles, for some mysterious reason it had not been drained when the plantation was established some five years before. A shooting syndicate paid a hefty fee for the privilege of having their dogs scratched and pricked by the undergrowth in a vain attempt to raise some game.

The plantation remained a favourite sanctuary for pheasants, and was deserted for the rest of the year except in late December. Then in early dusk the odd stealthy figure could be discerned poaching a Christmas tree.

That July, though, the apparent inefficiency of the wood owners was paying off. Undrained, the plantation remained moist and healthy.

Another sign of the severity of the drought was that our local store, the Midland Seeds Suppliers, was selling plastic rainwater butts. They did not normally stock them, but Midland Seeds was a good barometer to measure shortages by. They did not stock sugar until the shortage in 1974, nor salt. But it quickly had supplies of both. When all the normal suppliers of charcoal ran low for two months in 1975, Midland Seeds had plenty. Now all the garden centres had given up hope of obtaining water butts from wholesalers, but the front of the Midland Seeds Suppliers shop abounded with them. These were, of course, expensive – 50 per cent more than two years before.

Worrying about water now dominated our lives. Tanker deliveries had become so unreliable and irregular that we were often short of unpolluted drinking water. We were still pumping a little water out of the well, but it was so contaminated that even after boiling it tasted peculiar. It gave coffee and tea a particularly vile flavour, as if the cups had not been properly washed-up.

We had gone through the stages where the shortage had meant just inconvenience, and then sacrifices. Now we often felt we could not go on much longer. To get through each day was a matter of constant planning. One morning I was totally preoccupied by the water problem. Once again there was nothing for the stock to drink, and no water for use in the house. Rain had been forecast for the previous night but had not arrived; nor had the tanker promised by the Water Authority. Immersed in my anxiety I forgot to shut up our alsatian, who bit the postman. I arrived on the scene in time to see him cuss the dog, leap into his van and disappear down the road in a cloud of dust.

No crime in the country quite equals a dog attacking the postman, for the men who deliver our mail play a crucial role in communications in scattered, isolated communities. Apart from collecting and distributing all the gossip along with the mail, they also run a very real social service, doing things like picking up prescriptions for the elderly.

When Tom was away from home, jumping the horses at shows, Harry, the Welsh postman, always hooted his horn and waited to see that all was well with me.

It is not only the injury from a dog bite that is infuriating, but the inconvenience. It means the postman interrupting his round to go down to the cottage hospital for an anti-tetanus injection. Then he has to fill in numerous forms in triplicate for a new uniform to replace the one ripped up by some over-enthusiastic jaws. And we had given that postman enough trouble already.

When we had moved into the farm it was one of the conditions of sale that the boundary should be fenced immediately. We were too busy putting windows in the house to do more for the first two weeks than, as a temporary measure, tack up two strands of barbed wire. Not having a spare gate we slung the two strands of wire across the road as a makeshift gate that had to be unwound from the fence post. Unaware of this new obstacle the postman drove straight through it one morning and ripped off his wing mirrors.

Fearing terrible repercussions, perhaps a court case ending in a death sentence for our alsatian, I awaited the postman's visit the next day with trepidation. But he had swallowed his wrath, and blamed it all on the weather. I promised contritely that the dog would be shut up when he called in future.

Towards the end of July we got some relief from the depressing monotony of round-the-clock work and round-the-clock water-carting. It was not in the form of extra water but of an additional pair of hands. Morag's boyfriend, Ian, called in on the way back to Scotland from Devon and decided to stay a week and help us get in the straw harvest.

We were perversely cheered by his news that the situation in the West Country was bad too. In Plymouth all drinking water had to be boiled because supplies were so low there was danger of contamination. There was even less grass there than around us; almost all farmers were feeding full winter rations of hay and corn to their dairy cows. Those lucky enough to have mains water still had adequate supplies, but farmers with private resources were saddled with the same burden of carting water as we were.

But actually living without water was a new experience for Ian. 'Och, it's really opened my eyes to the drought,' he said after the first day. 'I'd read about it, and I'd seen how dry everything is, but it's a different world when you actually have to go as short as this.

'Do you know, I flushed the loo without thinking yesterday. Och, I cussed myself. You would never have thought a little thing like that could be so important.'

The straw harvest is now one of the busiest weeks of the year. Yet before 1974 it never figured on our farming calendar. Hay was cheap and readily available. There was no call for straw for fodder, only litter. Much of it was left to be burned. Livestock farmers who did not grow enough winter fodder on their own holdings could buy hay straight off the field for around £10 a ton.

The great grain drain from the United States to Russia in 1973 changed all that. The Russian coup in cheaply buying up American grain when their own harvest failed meant corn prices, and with them hay prices, spiralled. These went to about £30 a ton that winter. After the wet summer of 1974 the price climbed to £50 a ton and then £70 and over.

Farmers looked to the past for the answer to their winter feeding problems. They recalled the old nursery rhyme:

> Hay is for horses,
> Straw is for cows,
> Milk is for little pigs,
> And wash for old sows.

Oat and barley straw began to be fed, particularly to beef cattle, instead of hay. Naturally the price of straw increased – from about £3 a ton to about £25. But it was possible to buy it 'behind the combine', bale it yourself and cart it for £10 a ton. Along the motorways truck after truck could be seen conveying straw from East Anglia to the dairy farmers of the West Country.

Even with Ian's help the straw harvest was no picnic. One problem was that the baby had to come with us. He could not be left alone at the farm. We had bought the straw from a twenty-acre field about half a mile away. We had to bale it there, and carry it home. On the outward journey the baby rode on the trailer strapped in his pushchair. On the way back he sat on my knee as I drove the tractor, while his pushchair topped off the load. This was all strictly against the safety regulations, but we had no alternative.

The second problem was the heat in the bays of the corrugated-iron dutch barns, where we were stacking the straw. There it was as hot as the blast from a suddenly opened oven door. The temperature was well over the one-hundred mark. As the bay filled up and the air-space decreased it became impossible to work for more that fifteen minutes at a time. Sweat poured down our faces and into our eyes, and coursed down our bodies, making rivulets in the dust on our skin.

The sweat combined with the dust – there seemed to be as much dust in the bales as straw – to form a grimy paste which worked its way into our joints at our elbows and behind our knees. Washing never seemed to remove it all and the paste rubbed our skin sore. We longed for a bath every night when we had finished for the day, but for that there was certainly not enough water.

Only at the end of the week, after we had lugged and stacked 2500 bales, did we allow ourselves a bath. At least Tom and I shared the water of one bath, Morag and Ian that of another. But the two Scots seemed to thrive on shared adversity. At the end of the week they got engaged.

11. August 1976 (I)

The July days slipped into August, and still there was no sign of the heat-wave ending. Britain was now heartily sick of the drought. After six weeks of cheerfully accepting the new climate people started to complain. The heat brought a monotony to life that had never existed in the changeable summers of the past. We are notorious for our national preoccupation with the weather but its very unpredictability adds a stimulating uncertainty.

The long-range weather forecast held out no hope at all; for the next thirty days we were in for higher than average temperature and lower than average rainfall.

Around the farm the protective circle of woodland shimmered gold and red above combine harvesters busy reducing the wheat fields to stubble. In the west Midlands the harvest was proving to be unexpectedly good, with yields of winter wheat, barley and oats near the average. It was a different story in the south-east; there, yields were down as much as 50 per cent.

Fruit crops were badly affected. In the west Midlands the fruit was so small most of it could only be used for processing. Egg production was down because the hot weather put the hens off laying.

Over one hundred flower shows at fêtes throughout the country were cancelled because of the drought. The exhibits were just not up to standard. Commercial horticulturalists had their problems too: a mystery disease was attacking leeks. A fungus in the forests, which thrived because of the mild winter, was killing off silver birches by the thousand.

In Devon the farmers' plight was so desperate that the local

National Farmers' Union asked its headquarters in London to see, if our Government could do nothing, whether the Common Market Council of Ministers could help. They suggested Britain should appeal for aid for dairy and arable men in the south, south-east and Exeter areas. In Devon some farms had received only a quarter of an inch of rain since March.

In Somerset huge wall maps were drawn up at the local authority's headquarters showing all known sources of water. Farmers who ran dry could consult them to find their nearest alternative supply. The Milk Marketing Board was using its milk tankers to deliver water to farms in isolated areas.

In Lincolnshire farmers were being advised to provide storage capacity for water for the 'considerable possibility' that supplies would cease completely in some areas. There was already a voluntary ban there on irrigation. Where crops needed only an inch of rain to reach maturity irrigation was allowed, but where they needed more water no irrigation was permitted at all.

The effects of the drought were already beginning to hit housewives. Vegetables were scarce and expensive. In our local town one of the greengrocers stopped selling new potatoes altogether. Because of the drought the skins would not rub off as they normally do, and no one wanted to pay 20p a pound for marble-sized spuds that had to be peeled. Some of the keen gardeners in Micklebury who had kept their vegetable plots alive by dowsing them with waste or pond water were finding it profitable to sell their surplus produce in the local market.

Our own kitchen garden held no surplus. The runner-bean crop on which we relied to fill the freezer for winter meals ran to three individual beans. Joady reckoned it was so dry there was no nectar in the bean flowers and the bees were not pollinating them. One of Micklebury's beekeepers confirmed this; he had taken to feeding his bees with sugar because they were not finding enough nectar.

We were lucky to have a small crop of new potatoes, though they came in some weird shapes. Some were dented while others were 'granny spuds' with a little head on top.

Yet nature was trying to correct the balance. Hot-weather crops like sweet corn and outdoor tomatoes were thriving. Courgettes fruited like science-fiction monsters; every fruit we cut was replaced the next day by three even larger ones.

But if our vegetable crop was indifferent the rest of the farm was in better shape than we had dared hope. There was still some nourishment left for our cattle in the bleached dried grass that had managed to survive in patches. For most of our neighbours the problem of the shortage of grass was acute. As a result cattle, desperate for food, were breaking through fences, even if these were made of three strands of barbed wire. It was nothing unusual to drive through Micklebury and be confronted with a frantic steer in the road searching for fresh pastures.

Most of the farmers tolerated their neighbours' stock rampaging across their land. In a closely knit community like Micklebury they did not get up in arms about such things when life was so difficult for everyone. Jack Dalton, one of our next-door neighbours, gave up any hope of containing his sheep when the drought reduced his pasture to a moonscape. However often they were chased back, and however often the gaps in the hedges were repaired, the ewes and their lambs would break out again. By August they roamed freely over four adjoining farms. 'Dalton, him be gone in fer ranching,' was Micklebury's acceptance of this phenomenon.

The community operated a sort of knock-for-knock policy. In the case of minor damage by a neighbour's stock the sum went down on an invisible ledger to be cancelled by a favour at some future date. There were a few farmers, though, who operated outside this obligation bank. I met the wife of one of them in the post office.

'John Blake's cattle were in our corn this morning,' she said vehemently. 'I'm just off home to give him a piece of my mind. Time was when a beast only had to set foot on your land and you could have them on their insurance. Well, I can tell you, we're going to get something out of John Blake this time.

'If a man hasn't enough grass for his cattle and he can't keep them fenced in, he shouldn't be farming. What would happen if we all went on like that?

'Do you know,' she went on, her eyes glinting. 'I think there should be a central organization. When people don't farm properly they should have their land taken away from them and it should be let to people who can farm it. Then young people like us would have a chance to act on.'

The other customers heard her in silence.

We had a new and welcome visitor, a Japanese student who had advertised in the *Farmers' Weekly* for a place to stay for a month's working holiday. Her name was Meno. When she rang to make the final arrangements she asked: 'There is one thing, please. I would like to have a bath or a shower every day.'

I was completely floored, reluctant to cast myself in the role of a mean employer unwilling to let someone have access to the bath more than once a week.

I tried to explain. 'It's like this. You can spend as much time as you like in the bathroom, within reason. But the only thing is there isn't much water. There's a very severe water shortage in this part of the country. If you can bath in a bucketful you are welcome to have one every day.'

'You have no shower?' Meno was obviously astonished.

I replied we had not. I did not add that showers were almost unknown in rural Herefordshire. To most residents they were something out of the twenty-first century, an inadequate and new-fangled substitute for a real bath.

'You can always soap yourself all over and then rinse off with jugsful of water as everyone else in the house does.'

'OK,' she answered in a bewildered voice.

We awaited her arrival with trepidation. 'What do we do if her religion demands that she bathes daily?' queried Tom. 'If that's so we'll have to find a bit extra for her somewhere. Don't forget that was the case with the Pakistani students in Devon.'

But we were anxious for her to come. Any extra help at that time was invaluable, particularly as we were about to start our next round of straw-hauling, this time of wheat straw for litter.

'Don't say anything about the water coming from the well,' Tom said. 'It might put her off.'

Meno took it all in her stride. Despite her city background she took instinctively to the country life. She ate heartily and was soon chucking bales of straw up into the barn with the rest of us. Within a day of her arrival she poked her head into the well and asked if the water came from there.

'We-el, er-yes,' I admitted. 'Some of it. But the well doesn't give enough because of the dry weather. Some is delivered in a tanker. The county is very short of water.' To drive the point home I added: 'In some places they turn the water off at night to save it.'

'It is the same in Japan,' she said happily. 'There is no water, then the taps run dry.'

By now the British population was clearly divided between those with water and those without it. Those with water seemed blissfully unaware of the real implications of the drought. A friend who lived in the Thames Valley area, where a hose-pipe ban was introduced as late as 24 July, wrote woefully: 'If this drought goes on I just don't see how I can keep my rhododendrons alive much longer. Until the hose-pipe ban came in I had the sprinkler on them every evening. Now I have to carry water in buckets from the tap. I must have done fifteen journeys today from the tap to the garden with a bucket in each hand.'

The main confrontation in Micklebury between the 'haves' and the 'have nots', the watered and the unwatered, took place at the local guest-house, the Old Rectory. It normally had about fifteen guests at the height of the summer season and was run with cheerful efficiency by Mrs Baker and her husband, who had come to Herefordshire ten years before.

The Old Rectory's water came from a thirty-five-foot-deep well. Most of the time it held eighteen feet of water but by June 1976 it was down to seven feet – a foot lower than ever recorded in the verbal annals of local history.

Faced with the prospect of a guest-house without water and hence without guests, the Bakers' morale was further lowered by the prediction of their farming neighbour. 'You'll be out. Your well will run dry afore the end of the summer,' he assured them confidently as the season's bookings began to roll in.

As it turned out it was the farmer who came off worse in the drought. It was his well that ran dry. He decided to have it deepened. When that happened his pond disappeared. All the water in it drained into the well as though the plug had been taken out.

By the time the first guests of the season set foot in the Old Rectory, the Bakers had worked out a pattern of strict water economies. The new washing-up machine, purchased to lighten the toil of the expanding business, stood in the kitchen untouched by human hand, unfilled by dirty dishes.

The guests were asked to co-operate. A new set of rules was added to the house regulations. Showers were permitted but all baths were banned. At the beginning of June a large notice appeared in the lounge: IN VIEW OF THE WORSENING WATER SITUATION IT WOULD BE MUCH APPRECIATED IF GUESTS COULD PLEASE MANAGE WITH ONE SHOWER PER PERSON PER WEEK. WE DO SINCERELY REGRET ANY INCONVENIENCE. It was couched as a request but Mr Baker saw to it that one shower per week was the limit.

From then on the notices proliferated. In the bedrooms guests were asked to be as economical as possible with water. They were told to put the plug in the basin before running the tap. In the lavatory they were requested not to flush unless they had to. 'I sometimes think that one is a mistake,' Mr Baker remarked wearily one blistering August afternoon.

On arrival most guests seemed happy to put up with the inconvenience after Mrs Baker had explained the situation. But when they came up against what a water shortage really meant their patience was apt to wear thin.

Within twenty-four hours many had changed their tune. 'Can't we just have a tiny bath?' they pleaded. 'The whole family will share the same water.' And if it did rain for about quarter of an hour they said eagerly, 'We can have a bath now, can't we? It'll be all right for a bit. It's rained.'

One family of four was quite determined to have a bath. 'We must all have a bath every day,' demanded the mother. Mr Baker was intransigent. Two days later they had another try. 'I've got a bad hip. I must have a bath for medical reasons.' Mr Baker was unmoved. That night there was the sound of cases being packed. In the morning the family went home – not to a water-rich county but to a West Country where the conditions were now worse than with us.

Mr Baker found the drought an interesting lesson in human behaviour. 'My basic observation is that people want their own way. They won't be diverted from what they want whatever the reason. People want a bath because they've always had one and they always will have one even in the Sahara Desert and even if they have to have a dust bath.'

Another inconvenience was the grass tennis court. It was so dry it resembled a hard court. Guests could not understand why the Bakers did not turn the sprinklers on. 'It's not like this at home,' they complained.

More trouble came over the trout stream. Free fishing for

guests was advertised in the brochure but when guest arrived there were no trout and very little stream. It was the Bakers' fault. The whole water shortage was the Bakers' fault. 'Why is there going to be a milk shortage?' several guests asked. They could not understand that cows produce milk from lush grass and water, and that without both less milk is produced.

Not all the guests were so clueless. One elderly woman from the north of England refused water at meals to help the economies. Another guest, who begged the Bakers not to give him away, was a highly placed official in one of the West Country water authorities. He had no hope of escaping the drought and after a week was recalled to his job.

The Bakers survived the drought. Mr Baker said afterwards: 'We got everything screwed down. They didn't even get a full glass of water at meals. There were no jugs on the table. I went round filling all the glasses.'

In fact many of the Bakers' guests found the drought on their own doorsteps when they returned home. At the end of July the water shortage was ceasing to be a minor local matter afflicting parts of the West Country and south Wales. It became a major problem for half of Britain. London and the Thames Valley area introduced a hose-pipe ban near the end of July. In Herefordshire itself consumers were told to cut consumption by 15 per cent or the taps would be turned off in some areas for one or two nights a week. Over in the east Midlands householders were told stand-pipe rationing was only a matter of a week or two away.

In Northamptonshire the situation sounded chaotic. There were not enough stand-pipes for every street. The Water Authority planned to ration their use so that water would only be available at certain times.

'How will the old people manage?' a friend in the east Midlands asked me. 'I can't see them queueing up at the stand-pipes with their plastic buckets.'

'They will,' I assured her. 'They'll just have to. They've been doing it in this part of the world for months.'

Rationing also raised the serious question of health problems. In Northamptonshire members of the local health committee were recalled from holiday for an emergency meeting. Not only was there the danger of disease from unflushed lavatories and less frequently washed hands. There was also the real possibility of a epidemic of something like typhoid because people were drinking water from long-abandoned and contaminated wells.

In the correspondence columns of the national newspapers there was a lively discussion about the possibility of opening up old wells.

Most of the old houses in the country areas had a well and it was suggested that if they were opened up they would make a useful contribution to Britain's dwindling water resources. The proponents of this idea seemed to overlook the possibility that such wells, like the country's rivers and bore-holes, were likely to be empty. Many people did unearth their old wells but many of those that did contain water were found to be polluted.

On the farm our own water shortage took yet one more turn for the worse at the beginning of August. Tanker deliveries to private homes stopped again. This time it was because the tanker used for such trips failed its MOT test.

That decided us. Cost what it might, we would go onto the mains. We could not face another year like this. I remembered the plea of the Water Authority in the spring that anyone not on the mains should get connected. A second dry winter was being forecast so there seemed no alternative but to borrow the money and put the farm on the mains. It was that or selling up.

The first step was to get an estimate of the cost. We contacted the Water Authority about the possibility of water from the Micklebury main reaching the farm. On the third request, an official came up to measure the pressure. When he rang with the answer Tom was out, so it was left to me to play a vigorous game of bureaucratic ping-pong.

The pressure in the village supply was 140 feet and we were at 150 feet above Micklebury. The official concluded: 'So I don't think we can get the water up to you. Good-bye.'

'Wait a minute,' I protested. 'Does "think" mean you definitely can't?'

'Ah well, there's always the possibility they could open the pressure valve in the main.'

'Who's they?'

'The powers that be.'

I tried another tack. 'If the water can't get up here of its own accord, surely we could install a pump to help it on its way? A ten-foot shortfall is nothing for an ordinary commercial pump, most will push water up to twenty-five feet.'

But he had an objection to that. 'Then you'll need a pressure chamber somewhere on the hill to your farm. And that,' he said with a flourish, 'would be very expensive. Good-bye.'

'Now hang on. What's wrong with an ordinary tank with a ball-cock at the highest point the water will flow? Then we can pump it up from there.'

That was game, if not set, to me. 'It's funny you should say that,' he replied. 'You know Mr Gordon on the Worcester Road? He keeps horses like you and that's how they get water from the main.'

'At what point should we put the tank?' I insisted.

'Now that's another department. You must ring our Mr Cousins.'

And there the ball stopped. Tom rang Mr Cousins but further play had to be delayed until we had applied in writing for a connection to the main. Only then would they tell us where to put the half-way tank. When we asked for an application form Tom was told: 'You know we are not making any new connections because of the drought. Orders from Brecon.'

This seemed to us a clear enough contradiction of the Government's stated policy that agriculture should have priority where supplies were restricted. Our view was confirmed by a Ministry of Agriculture adviser when he came up to tell us about grants towards the cost of a connection.

But he too introduced some new snag. In the first place the payment of the grant would be delayed for three months. Drought or no drought, this was one of the Government's spending cuts, as announced the previous month. Then the adviser added: 'The grant won't apply to you anyway, I'm afraid. The Water Boards in the West Midlands aren't making any new connections, so no grant applies. I know of two farms that have been turned down already – one in the Severn–Trent area and the other in the Welsh Water Authority area.'

'Then what's all this about priority for agriculture? Does the Ministry in Whitehall know what's going on down here?'

'They know all right,' he answered sadly. 'It's one of those things that gets swept under the carpet.'

Baffled, without tanker deliveries and without any hope of

getting on the main, we turned to our ally in the local health department. Even he could not persuade the Water Authority to resume tanker deliveries or to give us a mains connection. But he told us not to give up hope. 'I believe both decisions to be unlawful. They have a responsibility to supply all people with water, not just existing customers. Our hands are tied. But individual members of the public can do something. You can contact your Member of Parliament and get him to bring pressure on the Water Authority.

So we put in our application to go onto the mains, and enlisted Leominster's MP, Peter Temple-Morris, to help us in our fight both for tankers and for the mains. He had no luck with the tanker deliveries, but he added our case to those already pressing the Ministry of Agriculture to do something about demanding emergency mains supplies for farms without water.

In the end it was not the Water Authority that rescued us. It was the local chocolate factory. After a week with no water for the house, except a little from the well, I rang the authority for the seventh time. Morag was suffering from a stomach bug which could have been the result of drinking polluted water. She wanted to have a bath before she went to the doctor and there just was not enough water.

As on the previous seven days no tanker was available. The official explained: 'It's all the Ministry of Transport's fault. All the other tankers are at Ross filling the reservoir. We should be exempt during the drought like the fire brigade and the ambulance service.'

'We must have some water,' I shouted at him.

'I don't know what you can do, my dear. I really don't. But I did hear Kem's, the Cadbury transport people, were delivering water. It's Bodenham. I haven't got the number but I know it's Bodenham something.'

Trembling with excitement I found the number in the book, rang the transport manager and explained the situation. I prepared myself for another disappointment. Insteady his reply was as welcome as if a real downpour had suddenly started.

'Yes, we can let you have a tanker in two hours. Don't worry about paying, we'll invoice you in the normal way. Have a good bath.'

What no one at the Water Authority had bothered to mention

until then was that Cadbury's had instituted some time ago a
regular water delivery service. Its fleet of tankers normally ferried
milk from the farms to its milk chocolate factory near Leominster.
With the drop in milk production because of the drought some of
the tankers had been made idle. They were now being used to
carry much needed water to houses, farms and even factories in
the area. A jam factory had a standing order for eight loads a day.

Cadbury's did not have the equipment to pump the water into
our cisterns. Instead they piped it into the almost empty well.
Luckily it did not drain away. The tanker driver told us he had
filled a well on a hill the previous week. By the next morning all
the water had disappeared but an elderly woman living lower down
was delighted to find her well had refilled overnight.

Apart from Cadbury's more helpful attitude their tankers carried
more water – 2000 gallons – and it was cheaper. Provided we
could continue to pay we now had to hand a means of coping
with weeks more drought if need be.

We got our water on that day, 6 August. But for millions of
people in Britain, the day marked the start of severe restrictions
on water supplies. The new Drought Act became law, fifteen
months after the onset of the dry period, nine months after the
first reservoirs had run dry and five months after the urgent
warnings sounded by the water authorities. For two dry dusty
months precious water had sprinkled down on Britain's thirsty
parks and sports grounds. It had flowed down drains after washing
buildings and vehicles. It had topped up private swimming pools,
as water in them evaporated in the heat. Now – if somewhat late
in the day – the inessential uses of water could be banned, and
people could be fined up to £400 if they broke these bans.

The Government stopped talking about 'if' there is water
rationing; the word now was 'when'. Several water authorities
applied for orders under the new Act at once. In Plymouth more
than a quarter of a million families faced the prospect of their taps
being turned off. From September rationing was to start with one
stand-pipe in the street for every twenty houses. Barnstaple,
Bideford, Oakhampton and Tavistock were likely to follow suit.

Leeds faced similar restrictions. To help alleviate the shortage
the South-Western Water Authority was constructing emergency
pipelines to divert supplies from water-rich areas to drought-
stricken ones.

Herefordshire was still regarded as being quite well off for water. The Welsh National Water Development Authority announced it was to seek an order to impose rationing, but would delay implementing it if consumers could achieve the necessary saving – about 15 per cent – themselves. Some areas including Hereford, but not Leominster, were threatened with one night a week without water and possibly two if the situation became worse.

Other regional authorities were casting around for less conventional solutions. The Wessex Water Authority, which covers Avon, Somerset, Dorset, most of Wiltshire and parts of Gloucestershire and Hampshire, wrote to the Department of Cloud Physics in New South Wales asking for information on rainmaking. But there seemed little chance of easing the situation by seeding clouds with dry ice pellets or lining them with silver dioxide to induce rain. The clouds had to be the right height and of a special type. There was also the problem that while rain might be a godsend for farmers and industry, it could spell disaster for other people. Who would be responsible for any flooding that might result? Who would pay compensation for washed out agricultural shows and ruined seaside holidays? As the problem with which we had lived for so long now became the nation's problem, we followed with fascination the drought reports which began to fill the newspapers and crowd the television screen.

12. August 1976 (II)

By the middle of August there were times when we would be engulfed by a real fear that the rain would never come, that the climate had changed for ever. But for the holidaymakers it was marvellous. Visitors arriving at the Bakers' guest-house would say with shining eyes: 'Isn't this weather lovely? I do hope it lasts just this week.' The Bakers had reached the stage where they could not trust themselves to answer.

As we hauled water, went unwashed and watched the grass die out, we wondered if there had been a fundamental change in the climate and the wet summers of the past had gone for ever. Just because Britain had previously enjoyed a damp climate, it did not follow that it would in the future. After all, the North African deserts were once the grain bowl of the Roman Empire.

It was an eventuality that hit me hard one evening when the vet came up to the farm to treat a bullock with pneumonia. After he had given it an injection we leant on the gate, by then rickety with the heat, studying the rest of the cattle nosing around for nourishment on the bare ground. He asked me if they had been drenched recently for worms. 'Larval activity has been very low this year because of the dry weather. When it rains they will come to life and I'm expecting a massive outbreak of worm infestation.'

It had been so long since anyone had talked about 'when' the rain comes and so long since we had done anything in expectation of rain, that I was taken by surprise.

The vet's confidence was quite inspiring. I said: 'Do you really think it will ever rain again? The weathermen are talking about another dry autumn and dry winter. In the papers some amateur forecaster was reported to have said the dry spell will last until 20 September.'

'Well, I suppose it must rain sometimes,' he answered. 'Even though there are times when I begin to think it won't. I've never known England like this; some sort of cycle seems to have been interrupted.'

The next day I went outside Herefordshire for the first time in three months, driving over to the cash and carry warehouse in Gloucester to do the grocery shopping for the next six months.

Once again the permanence of the drought hit me. The countryside was a scene of eerie devastation: mile upon mile of scorched bare fields. It looked as though a conquering army had swept through the county laying waste everything in its path. There was nothing but barren brown grass, only occasionally relieved by a green patch of maize or potatoes. Every mile or so was a length of charred hedgerow where a carelessly thrown cigarette end had completed the burning up process. Cattle were bunched in orchards. Paddocks were stained with the mess of manure and loose hay that comes with hand feeding.

Herefordshire was dry, but Gloucestershire was decaying. To the drought was added in Gloucestershire the damage of dutch elm disease. Herefordshire is a county of oaks and beeches. Gloucestershire is elm country. Perhaps it was the skeletal outline of the dead trees, ravaged for five years now by the disease, that added the final strokes of doom to the picture. The twigs at the end of the branches seemed like a million hands reaching up to the heavens for rain.

It was on this drive that I felt as if the doomsday predicted by the environmentalists had arrived. The whole scene seemed to demonstrate how easily our highly sophisticated civilization can be brought to its knees. Farmers talk of stocking ratios, units of nitrogen fertilizer per acre and other developments of the scientific age. The Government produces White Papers about increasing production. Yet without a measure of co-operation from the elements, these efforts are completely wasted – are indeed destructive. This summer the elements had withdrawn that co-operation. Now not only agriculture but also industry faced disruption. Decades of industrial unrest might prove as nothing compared to the damage the hostility of the elements could cause in a few short months.

The drought had even influenced the pop scene. The car radio picked up a song high in the charts, called 'Rainmaker' with the refrain 'Make it rain, make it ra-in'. It echoed what we all felt, as our nerves and our patience became ever more stretched. One Sunday morning they played 'Jerusalem' on the radio. I suddenly found myself in tears. 'Will we ever see this as a green and pleasant land again?' I asked Tom with something close to despair.

We had to face the fact winter would be with us soon and we wondered how we would possibly cope then. In winter the climate is our enemy. It must be fought day in and day out. Stock must be guarded against the illnesses brought by the cold and damp. Nature's deficiencies in providing food for only six months of the year must be countered by storing and handing out vast quantities of fodder and corn for the cattle. And much of the fighting is done in miserable conditions, when you struggle through mud which seems intent on dragging the Wellingtons from your feet. You feel frozen to the marrow inside layers of restricting vests and sweaters.

In the spring and summer the climate is normally our ally. We expect grass and crops to come to life and the days to be long and warm. But the summer of '76 was worse than the most severe winter; it took our water and burnt up our land and our spirit. To grapple with a hard but dry winter on top of such a summer seemed too much. Yet that was the outlook.

Even the Government was expecting the dry weather to continue for many months. It asked Lord Nugent, head of the National Water Council, to come up with some contingency plans by October.

Day by day throughout August the drought spread and water restrictions tightened. Millions of people in cities and towns in England and Wales were affected as the water pressure in the taps was lowered. In south-east Wales water was turned off for twelve hours at night. Shops ran out of buckets. Rationing, it was announced, was to be introduced in the middle of October in Northamptonshire, parts of East Anglia and Leicestershire.

Surprisingly, north Norfolk, one of the driest areas, was hardly affected by the restrictions. Its water was supplied by a private enterprise operation which had sunk extra bore-holes some years earlier in anticipation of an exceptional drought. Hose-pipes in the area were banned in August, not because water was short, but after appeals from the state Water Authority to standardize restrictions in the county.

In the West Country officials warned that the two million people who take late holidays in Devon and Cornwall in September might have to be told to stay at home because there would not be enough water for them. Ireland offered to send Britain water but the suggestion was turned down because the cost of ferrying it across the Irish Sea was too high.

A man in Kidderminster was fined for performing a witch-doctor dance in the nude. It rained there within twenty-four hours.

Around us in Herefordshire the townspeople were being urged to adopt the techniques we had learned the hard way across the past two years. The Welsh National Water Development Authority took half a page in the local newspaper to spell out: WATER IS SHORT. SAVE NOW OR SUFFER LATER. The public was advised to have a stand-up bath or shower, or to bath in only two or three inches of water; to wash-up only once a day and to use the waste water to flush lavatories, and only to flush them to dispose of solid matter. But I never met or heard of anyone with mains tap water who paid much heed to the suggestions.

To hammer home the message the Water Authority's announcement was illustrated with a picture of women queueing up at a water tanker with buckets. It was curiously old-fashioned. The women wore pinnies and headscarves and carried enamel or galvanized buckets. I suspect it was a photo taken during the blitz.

In Hereford itself, the hospitals were taking precautions in preparation for water rationing. At the County Hospital an exercise was carried out to see how they would cope if the supply was cut off at night. As the water shortage worsened the staff took the precaution of filling all the baths with water at night. In the morning the unused water went down the plug-hole.

Wasting water in public was another matter. A tanker continued to water the flowers by Hereford's Roman Wall. But it displayed a sign announcing: 'This is not mains water'.

At the Withington Horticultural Show a tanker watered the track used for the stock-car racing to lay the dust. Over the public address system came the explanation: 'This water is unfit for human or animal consumption. It is stagnant water from a disused canal.'

In Leeds a woman caught watering her garden at midnight was fined £5, with £25 costs. She refused to pay up because she claimed it was a lot of fuss about a little bit of water. In Leominster a man seen by a Water Authority official watering his lawn with a hose-pipe was not taken to court. Instead the furious official told him: 'I'd like to wrap that hose-pipe round your neck so you couldn't even drink the water you're depriving other people of.' We reckoned the most suitable punishment for these offenders would have been a week on our farm carting water.

In parts of north Devon there was an outcry when people were accused of ignoring requests to save water. They had been asked to cut consumption by half – from fifty gallons a head a day to twenty-five gallons. The actual response was a meagre saving of between 10 and 15 per cent. Areas saving the least were to be punished by being the first to get stand-pipe rationing. Residents blamed holidaymakers who, they said, gaily washed their cars and took huge baths while everyone else scrimped and saved.

At that time, the middle of August, our old friend Joady ran out of water. His eighty-foot bore-hole packed up. He was a different man from the confident forecaster who had stopped to chat when Tom had been drawing water down by the Hopkinses' farm. He no longer greeted Tom with his usual bantering, 'Not still short of water, eh?' No conjunctions of moons had availed even Joady against this relentless sun.

National Farmers' Union officials toured the desert-dry farmlands of the south-west and then asked the Government for help. They wanted a revaluation of the 'green pound', the Common Market unit of account for agricultural prices; grants for re-seeding burnt pastures; and a change in the tax laws to allow farmers to spread the cost of the drought over three years.

The Minister of Agriculture, Mr Fred Peart, took a whistle-stop tour round the badlands to see for himself. He was sympathetic but held out little hope for substantial Government aid. Dairy farmers warned they would not have enough fodder to feed their stock through the winter. Because of the drought practically all butter production in England and Wales would have to stop at the end of August.

It was the prospect of an increase in beer prices that warranted the biggest headlines. The dry weather had pushed up the nitrogen content of much of the country's barley, making it unsuitable for brewing. As a result the price of malting barley went to over £90 a ton.

I never read any mention in the press of the most telling sight of all. Farmers had taken to grazing their sheep on roadside verges. Untouched by mechanical mowers because of local goverment spending cuts, the verges often had the only grass left in southern Britain. As we drove along in the car we would see the occasional lonely figure with a dog and a dozen ewes making the most of this reserve. It must have been a long day for those farmers, guarding their sheep from the traffic. But they had no alternative if they wanted a good crop of lambs in 1977. The ewes had to be 'flushed' on good grass to bring them into season before they were put to the ram.

Cattle prices went down and down. 'If only we had the money and we knew the drought would end,' I said to Tom. 'We could buy a score of those red heifers that are going for a song and make a fortune.'

Some of our fellow farmers in Micklebury were forced by the shortage of grass to sell their cattle on the sliding market. Ben David came up one evening to buy a ready-made bow tie.

It may seem a strange object for small holders to stock but we held a supply. Tom had taken 107 of them as part of a deal for a horse. Barter is far from dead in the countryside, particularly in these days of inflation. After all the Germans hoarded cardboard cuffs during the Weimar Republic inflation. Unfortunately the best offer we had received for this odd lot was 10p each, so we had decided to hold onto them and sell them locally.

'You got any of those coloured sashes for round your waist?' asked Ben.

No, we had no cummerbunds. ' 'Fraid not. We can't rival Moss Brothers,' I replied. 'But why don't you have a green dicky bow as well as a black one? You can have two for the price of one Only £1. They're £2.50 in the shops.'

He chuckled and bought. He had arrived full of gloom about the weather. His father, he told me, had had to sell ten steers that day. They were six hundredweight animals and they had made an average of £125 each – less than £21 a hundredweight. If prices fell like that we were all in trouble.

If the humans and the domestic animals had had more than enough of the drought, the wildlife around the farm was flourish-

E

ing. There were rabbits everywhere. They came to feed not just at dawn and dusk but all day. We wondered where on earth they found water but rabbits are noted for being able to adapt to prolonged droughts.

Our terriers caught, and consumed, one apiece every day. Not that it was difficult for them. The rabbit colonies were so thick the dogs could hardly have missed just by running in a straight line down the field.

Another more indirect consequence of the dry weather was the enormous number of fleas the dogs picked up, apparently from the ever-increasing fox population. One evening two local CID officers came up to see us about a harness we had reported lost. Tom and I watched, transfixed with a mixture of horror and of laughter, as a flea moved unswervingly across the face of one of the policemen, coming out of his hair, running down his cheek and finally disappearing into a woolly sideburn.

The tropical heat also attracted some rare migrants from abroad. One sultry morning I was concentrating on washing-up the dishes in three inches of water when I glanced out of the kitchen window to see a strange-looking pigeon strutting up and down the yard. From time to time we play host to visiting racing pigeons which seek sanctuary on the farm during the sudden thunderstorms which punctuate normal summers. They stay for two or three days, keeping a beady eye on us from the safety of the roof and regaining their strength on corn we scatter for them. Then they are off, wings working overtime, as they belt back to a loft or backyard cage in the heart of some distant city.

But this time the dove was not the usual pastel-tinted racing pigeon. It was smaller, and with more exotic markings – a pinkish head and neck with a broad speckled black and copper collar. The edge of its wings were splashed with sapphire blue as though it had been marked by the sky on its long flight from its homeland. It was a palm dove, which the reference book in the library told us was a native of Africa and south-west Asia, although it now breeds in Europe and Asiatic Turkey.

Cadbury's kept us sane by continuing to deliver water regularly, even though the Water Authority dealt a further blow. Water could no longer be drawn from nearby Leominster, but only from two other places in the county, Hereford and Ross. It meant the tanker had to make a big detour to fill up, and then double back, making the journey thirty miles instead of sixteen. Cadbury's regretfully told us the charge would be £16 instead of £10.

When I rang the water authority to protest, I was told the level of the underground supply at Leominster was dropping while there was surplus water at Hereford.

The official drew me into a new debate by his reply: 'If the drought continues and supplies in the Leominster area run low we will be open to the criticism that we allowed non-consumers to draw off water and worsen the situation.'

I could not let that one pass. 'It may be news to you,' I countered, 'but we are all consumers. We all have a right to your water and we *have* to have water to keep our stock alive. There has been no mention of water restrictions being imposed in Leominster – not even for one night a week. Yet some of us have been surviving on far less water than the majority of people in this country have had for almost a year. Now you tell us we are going to have to pay even more for the drop we do use.'

'That may be so,' he answered. 'But that's the policy. We have to maintain supplies to our own consumers first.'

Others with private supplies did not fare much better. In the north of Herefordshire the country people without water had taken to bathing in a pool in the River Lugg to keep clean.

Newtown, the hamlet in the south of the county which had been without water since February, was still drawing its supplies from the well in the middle of a field. An ITN reporter visited it in the third week of August. 'News at Ten' showed the villagers ladling the brackish water into buckets. 'It's a bit dirty, isn't it?' asked the reporter.

The Newtonians were not disconcerted. 'Na. Give it time. It'll be all right when it settles.'

Newtown, we were told, was to receive an emergency supply the following week. A load of pipes arrived, as one resident put it, 'to keep us quiet'. By February 1977 they had been planted in the ground. It was in March 1977, over a year after the hamlet had first run dry, that mains water arrived at Newtown.

A real note of anxiety now crept into the predictions of the Government. London had ninety days' supply left, Leeds less than eighty days'. A million people in south-east Wales, already with no water for thirteen hours a day, had the cut-off period extended to seventeen hours. Their taps were dry from two in the afternoon until seven the next morning. In south Wales all but essential uses of water were firmly banned. There was no watering of parks, no topping-up of swimming pools. Commercial car washes put up the shutters. There was no cleaning of buildings and tap water could not be used for washing cars or watering gardens.

In the south-west a football club used the players' bath-water to water the goalmouth after the game. On the coast people were snapping up a special soap that lathered in salt water.

Near London a new scheme was opened to extract water by bore-holes from the aquifers 450 feet below Lambourne in Berkshire. The flow of the River Thames was reversed to prevent water from the lower tributaries being wasted by flowing away into the sea.

A similar scheme was got under way in Northamptonshire to reverse the flow of the River Ouse and to force water back into reservoirs, thereby providing for Northamptonshire and Bedfordshire the following summer.

On 23 August the Government made a move. It appointed Dennis Howell, the Minister of Sport, as Drought Minister. He described the situation as 'serious but not critical' and still refused to announce a state of emergency. He decided all the powers needed were already in the Drought Act. In the drought-stricken areas, four equal priorities were announced for water: industry, agriculture, health and safety, and essential domestic supplies – and that, said Mr Howell, meant drinking water.

All domestic consumers were asked to cut water consumption by 50 per cent. The slogan was: 'Every bucket of water saved now means one less an old-age pensioner will have to carry in a month's time'. Even the trade unions got in on the act with an appeal to 'save water or lose jobs'.

One of the first actions of the Minister was to set up a centre to which people could bring their drought problems. It quickly showed up one of the less pleasant sides of human nature. It became a snoop centre to which people could report their complaints about their neighbours. Mr Howell was shown on television taking the first call from the inquiring public. It was an angry householder complaining that a local riding stables was watering its schooling ring. That set the tone. More complaints followed, on the air and in the newspapers. The BBC joined in. 'Nationwide' took a relish in naming golf clubs which were

watering their greens, even when these claimed to have got permission from the water authorities. It recounted with glee how
householders had invaded one course and turned off the sprinklers.

The shortages mounted. On 27 August it was announced that
the source of the Thames, near Lechlade in Gloucestershire, had
dried up. The river itself was also leaking through its bed for a
four-mile stretch between the Eynsham and Days locks up-river
from Oxford. This had happened because the water table had
dropped. The Government asked people living in towns on the
banks of the Thames to stop putting waste water on their gardens
and to empty it down the drains so it could be recycled. Then
people living down river could use it – after treatment, of course.

By the end of August, the first worries arose about pollution.
The Department of Health had already issued a warning to doc-
tors to be on the alert for a disease in babies connected with high
nitrate levels in water caused by the drought.

It was a danger which farmers had already foreseen. Our
neighbour, John Hopkins, had his own unusual and disconcerting
thesis: 'River water is cleaned by filtering it through beds of
gravel. Then they add some chlorine to kill off the germs. But have
you ever heard of people being able to filter out liquids like cow
pee? No. They are usually left to be diluted by vast quantities of
river water.

'Cows pee up-river and little babies further down stream get
nitrate poisoning. They say it's because of the agriculture fertilizer in the river which isn't diluted as it normally is. But there
hasn't been any rain to wash the fertilizer off the fields into the
river. It's cow pee, and human pee, more concentrated than usual.'

It was all supposition, of course. But it was a disturbing
thought.

Still the dry weather went on. By now we noticed the dust more
than anything. The terriers only had to scurry round the yard in
play for clouds of the stuff to be wafted into the house. There
seemed to be no smell to anything anymore; the chalky dust in
our nostrils blocked out everything.

Fire was more of a danger than ever. Visitors were banned
from Forestry Commission woodlands in Shropshire and north
Herefordshire. Throughout the country efforts to fight forest
fires were hampered by water shortages and lowered pressure. By
the end of the summer the drought had cost the Forestry Com-

mission £1 million and 4500 acres of woodland had been destroyed.

Firing stubble was banned. We saw why when one local farmer took a risk and put a match to his fields. The result was astonishing; he apparently had a field of bare earth on fire. The ground was so dry that a deeply buried tree stump caught alight. For yards underground the old roots smouldered and as we walked across the field we could feel the heat of the earth and see the smoke rising up out of it.

Farmers had given up hope of ploughing their land after the harvest. The earth was so dry the fields were unworkable.

Furrows collapsed as heaps of dust. In some places tractors sank into the soil, their wheels spinning uselessly as they failed to get a grip on the powdery topsoil. Rollers, intended to flatten the soil, merely dragged it up in front of them like dust in front of a broom.

On 26 August the Sikh community in London imported a guru to pray for rain. That evening we went down to the black and white pub in Micklebury, the Fox and Pheasant, to replenish or supplies of Coke. For the first time for many months I caught a whiff of the fragrance of the flowers in the pub garden. More than that I could smell water.

'It's going to rain. I can smell it,' I told Tom.

Tom was cynical. 'You're always thinking it's going to rain. You're getting an obsession about it. We could get a month of this yet.'

On 28 August the rains came.

13. September 1976

The beginning of the end of the Great Drought in Herefordshire was a smattering of drizzle. It fell on Saturday, 28 August and reached us in the late morning. It was the harbinger of a wet British Bank Holiday weekend. The drought was to end in style.

As soon as we woke that Saturday morning we realized the long hot summer was over. No sunlight filtered through our bedroom curtains. When I looked out of the window the brown fields no longer shimmered under the early morning glare of a sun already pulsating with heat in a clear blue sky. Instead dark menacing clouds loomed over the bare countryside. They were moving in swiftly from the north-east packing the sky as if it would burst. This was not the usual direction for rain-bearing clouds – they chiefly come from the west and south-west – but there was no doubt about the weather's intention.

As the morning wore on it grew steadily darker, until the sky above us became a ceiling of unbroken slate. The atmosphere became more and more oppressive, charged with a feeling of both suspense and apprehension. In the countryside around us there seemed to be a lull in the buzz of life. A hush descended as if the world was holding its breath.

Then the rain came. At about half past eleven there was a slight sprinkling of rain for ten minutes. The dry spell was broken. Twenty minutes later there was another shower, heavier and longer. Then another and another. By the afternoon the rain was pelting down, pouring off the roofs and running in rivulets in the dust of the water-starved earth.

As we sheltered in the barn we could hear it drumming on the yard and shooting down the guttering pipes to thump into the rainwater tanks. To our ears it was superb music. Nature was celebrating the end of the worst drought in the history of industrial Britain with a grand percussion chorus.

No break in the dry spell had been forecast by the weathermen – the rain had moved in unexpectedly, but relentlessly, from Scandinavia. The Sikh community were quick to claim that it was all due to their guru. He had brought rain to London within twenty-four hours and to the rest of Britain within forty-eight hours. Scientists dismissed it as pure coincidence, but it made a cheerful point to gossip about.

Within a day our pastures were tinged with a faint water-colour green. Tiny hair-like spikes of grass were already beginning to thrust up through the mat of dead vegetation. It went on raining. All over Herefordshire there were heavy showers; the east of England was flattened by downpours. My sister in Northampton-shire phoned to share our delight and say that her globe artichokes had shot up three inches overnight.

More rain on Bank Holiday Monday washed out the local agricultural show. We ransacked dark cupboards for long-unused Wellingtons and anoraks. There was a particular problem with the baby – he had no shoes. He had started to walk in June and all through the dry summer days he had gone barefoot. We had been so busy surviving the drought there just had not been time to take him into town to buy shoes.

The first natural public reaction was that the rain must mean the end of the water shortage. When Tom went to collect water for the cattle several neighbours asked in amazement: 'Still cart-ing water? Hasn't all this rain put your well right?' It was an understandable misconception and one which the Water Council was anxious to correct. They were busy now with new warnings that even a whole winter of normal rainfall would not put things right.

The Meteorological Office predicted another dry month in its long-range forecast for September. By the end of the first week of the month it began to look as though they might be right for once and that our celebrations over the end of the drought had been premature. The days dawned clear and sunny once again as the temperature climbed back into the seventies. Grass stopped growing and the soil, which had soaked up the rain like a bone-hard sponge, looked as thirsty as ever. Firm springy turf gave way to gritty dust skating on hard earth.

We received a reply to our application for mains water from the Water Authority. It was a postcard with the comment: 'Your request has been received without prejudice.' We spent some time trying to figure out what that meant.

10 September – I ringed the day on my calendar – it rained again – and a day later stopped again. The dry weather returned, and in a particularly unpleasant form. Now it was cold as well as dry. We went at one stride from summer to a premature autumn. In the early mornings heavy dews nipped our feet with cold. Water dripped from the dying leaves on the hedgerows, and the summer foliage became a damp carpet under our boots. Evening mists crept up silently, and we rushed through the chores to find sanctuary in the warm kitchen.

Worst of all, the cold held back the growth of grass. Though our fields began to look greener, the grass did not grow vigorously, but looked meagre and unappetizing. There was nothing for it but to start feeding the cattle on full winter rations. We began to set out hay for them in the hope of bringing them into condition for selling. But on the first growth of the new grass they were actually losing weight in a way they had never done in the hot dusty days of the summer. The wet grass was going right through them, a digestive phenomenon which was only too obvious. As they galloped about streams of diarrhoea shot from their rear ends. The only way to improve matters would have been to bring them in at night for a feed of straw, to bind them up inside. But once we started shedding them at night we would have to go on doing so for the rest of the autumn, and we knew that housed cattle always fetch less in the market.

We decided that the best answer was to start selling the cattle a month earlier than usual. For the one bright spot was that by the beginning of September prices had jumped sharply. Throughout the summer farmers had been selling cattle as soon as they were fat enough for slaughter, in order to save spending money on feed. As a result, the normal 'autumn flush' of cattle into the market had not taken place. Fewer than usual were being offered for sale.

So on a wet cold autumnal day more reminiscent of November than Hereford's usual golden September, we took some of the remaining cattle to market. Things had changed a lot since the steamy July day when we had sold the first bunch. From the appearance of many of the cattle being auctioned it could have been midwinter. Instead of the fat, glossy animals that normally crush into the market after a summer at grass, the cattle which filled the pens were scraggy and rough-coated. Between the pens the concrete was awash with slushy manure. In the seats above the auction ring Joady's nephew was doing his profit and loss accounts as usual. It was cold and draughty despite the heaters; the seats were mucky with mud and manure from the boots of people sitting on the next tier up.

When our cattle stepped onto the scales at the entrance to the ring our fears about the deprivations of the summer were confirmed. In a normal summer they would have put on two and a half hundredweight. On average this year they had gained only one and a half hundredweight. We got a higher price than we had expected earlier in the year. This gave us some compensation, but even so we made £15 a head less on each beast than we had estimated at the start of the season.

But we were satisfied. We knew that the drought had cost some large-scale farmers thousands of pounds. The farming magazines and the newspapers had been full of reports of heavy losses. We considered we had got off lightly. After what seemed like long years of wasted time, we had now a chance of at least breaking even. We felt that life was definitely looking up. In July we had returned from our visit to market to face a long weary evening of water-carting. This time a pleasant surprise awaited us: in the middle of the dew-pond was a small puddle of water.

We were to have a further spell of anxiety, as the pundits continued to warn us that there were no real signs that the drought was sure to end. Then on 20 September the rains came once again. Rain hammered against the hard ground, and streamed off the roofs. All the rainwater tanks were now full to overflowing. The dew-pond soon held enough water to satisfy the thirst of our remaining cattle. The drain on supplies from our cistern tanks slackened. The levels in them remained surprisingly high, and we realized that the calves were drinking much less than in the summer. On 22 September we unloaded for the last time from the lorry the tanks we had used for collecting water. Our water carrier became a horse-box once again.

In the last ten days of September the weather warmed up. Around the farm the pastures grew completely green again. Suddenly the fields appeared to be full of tennis balls. As if to make up for the shortcomings of the summer, nature gave us, as well as the rest of Britain, a bumper crop of mushrooms. The high soil temperatures of the summer, coupled with plenty of rain, and the warm nights, had produced ideal growing conditions. For the first few days I struggled out of bed at six in the morning, spent an hour collecting mushrooms, and then drove into town to sell them to the butcher at 30p a pound. But the law of Too Much of a Good Thing soon caught up with me. One soon learns on a farm that unexpectedly high yields mean a glut on the market, which in turn means rock-bottom prices.

To make matters worse, the law of supply and demand does not always work as neatly in practice as in theory, especially in the case of food. According to the textbooks demand should recover as prices drop as the result of increased supplies. But sometimes demand actually falls when prices fall. This certainly happened in the Herefordshire market towns with mushrooms. The explanation was fairly simple. When the cheap mushrooms first appeared people rushed to buy them but after a couple of days of mushroom-filled plates they had eaten enough of them. On the farm we ate them three times a day – fried for breakfast and lunch and in a omelette for supper. But for most people they are basically a garnish, not a vegetable to eat at every meal.

So no one made much money out of the best mushroom crop within living memory. No system existed to get the crop to the big cities, and in the country towns and villages the greengrocers soon made it clear they did not want to know about mushrooms. People had stopped buying them. Prices flopped to 10p a pound. This was barely enough to cover the cost of picking and of the petrol needed to carry them to town. I put as many as I could into the freezer, and watched people in the greengrocers pay 20p for cabbage as the rest of our crop – no longer worth picking – was trampled underfoot by the cattle.

If for us the drought was over, for many people in the towns it was reaching its peak. We came in from our wet fields to watch on television or read in the paper reports of acute water shortages.

The ending of the drought posed a difficult problem for the water authorities. The heavy downpour on August Bank Holiday had naturally enough been taken as a sign that the worst was over. But we had only to look at the way the rain was bouncing and spluttering off our own concrete-hard pastures to know that it was going to take weeks before enough rain could seep through to the reservoirs, and make up for the losses not just of the summer, but of the previous years. Exasperatingly, the break in the drought came just at the moment when in many parts of the country severe restrictions were for the first time coming into force.

The east Midlands were warned that their water would be cut off at night from 8 September. In south Yorkshire stand-pipes were being installed, though a switch-off date had not been fixed. In north Devon, its population swollen by holidaymakers, supplies were cut off to homes in Tavistock, Barnstaple, Ilfracombe and some thirty other towns and villages, and stand-pipes were installed there in the streets. A last-minute report on the radio on the morning of switch-off day said that no cuts would be necessary, but this proved too optimistic and the stop-cocks were duly turned off. Hotels and business premises were excepted from these restrictions. This brought angry protests that holidaymakers were squandering water, and the chairman of the Water Council, Lord Nugent, was jeered and heckled when he visited Bideford. Plymouth was more fortunate. It was one city where an appeal for voluntary savings had worked. The residents cut their consumption by 40 per cent, and they avoided the worst.

South Wales appeared to be the hardest hit of the town areas. They had had a seventeen-hour daily switch-off for some time. This had cut consumption back, but with much inconvenience and hardship. When the schools resumed after the holidays children could attend only half a day. When the water was cut off at two o'clock in the afternoon, they were, for health reasons, sent home.

Wales was also the area where industry was most endangered by the shortage. A 50 per cent reduction in supplies to industry was planned for mid-September, unless it rained really heavily. Hard words began to fly back and forth. Welsh businessmen accused the officials of praying for rain all summer, instead of working on schemes to conserve supplies. They demanded that the good Welsh water of the north which was going to English cities should be made available to south Wales. They wanted a temporary rubber pipeline to be laid from the lakes of north Wales, or a fleet of road tankers used to haul the water overland. The Water Authority chief was rebuked by the Drought Minister for saying that life in south-east Wales could shortly come to a standstill.

The Government had, however, some soothing words for industry elsewhere in Britain. It said that most factories should get by, even if compulsory cuts had to be introduced, as four out of every five firms had their own supplies from rivers and bore-holes. These figures surprised us, for the rivers and bore-holes might themselves be running dry. One textile factory in Yorkshire had already closed because its private reservoir had dried up.

Meanwhile the shortages were producing their own legal wrangles. What constituted 'non-essential use', that requirement which was now being imposed even in relatively well-supplied areas like the north-west and the Thames Valley? Was it non-essential to use rainwater, or waste-water, to water your garden or wash your car? Yes, replied some authorities. No, said others – how can we tell that you are really using rainwater? So no wash-ing of cars at all became the rule in some places. But suppose this requirement brought you into conflict with the law in other ways? We followed with fascination the case of Mr John Dale-Glossop, a Cornish coach operator. Under the noses of two officials from the Water Authority he washed his coach inside and out to prepare it for the annual outing of a group of pensioners. He was taken to court for breaking the drought regulations. His solicitor pleaded that the Road Traffic Act laid down that coaches had to be clean inside and out, whatever the drought regulations might say. The magistrates dismissed the case, but Mr Dale-Glossop was left with £100 costs to pay.

September also saw some signs of significant activity in White-hall. The Government was planning seriously for the possibility of the drought lasting through the winter. The Navy was asked to prepare plans for shipping water to the south-west, perhaps from Norway. Idle oil tankers might be used, if they could be properly cleaned out. Another scheme was to use the milk trains which brought milk up from the West Country to carry water on their return journey. We noted with concern that the costs of all this would fall, not on the country at large, but on the consumers to whom it would be brought. Throughout September the

National Water Council kept up its campaign to save water. They took time on television. One advertisement showed a hand about to push down the handle on a lavatory cistern. 'Think before you flush', admonished the commentator. Other advertisements warned us that eighteen months of normal rainfall would be needed to replenish our water resources.

Then, in the last week of September, came the decisive break in the weather. On the night of Friday, 24 September, I was woken up by the noise of rain thundering onto our roof, and hitting the ground outside. When the day broke it broke on a downpour of tropical dimensions. The morning radio spoke of heavy rain across most of the country, and the forecasters talked now with real confidence of more to come. Indeed the morning news from deep in the West Country was already carrying the first evidence of the new vagary of the weather. In Polperro, we were told, rain and a high tide swelled a stream into a torrent, which surged through the village, drowned one old man, and wrecked homes and cars. Drought centres took on a new role – that of giving advice in flooded areas

Wearing waterproofs, we peered into the well. It held at least a foot of water. The rain was at long last seeping through the hard soil and reaching the underground reservoirs. So we declared that for us the drought was over. We abandoned at long last our self-imposed restrictions. It was baths for everyone, including the car, and the terriers with their fleas. All the kitchen reverberated with the sound of the ancient washing machine bumping and clattering as it dealt with mountains of curtains, chair covers and sweaters. Even the baby was allowed to play his favourite game – turning on the tap of the water butt.

By Sunday, 26 September the drought was everywhere on the retreat. The heavy rainfall of August Bank Holiday, and the patchy rainfall of the first three weeks of September had already proved to be twice that of normal years. A start had been made with re-filling the reservoirs and replenishing the natural underground reserves. There was of course still a long way to go. The September rain was to make up for only one-tenth of the rain which had not fallen earlier in the year. A further thirty inches of rain would be needed by March to restore the reservoirs and underground supplies to normal. Our own well was still only half full by the end of September, and our neighbour, Rivers, whose well was seventy-

feet deep, did not get enough water back into it for his supply to
be normal much before Christmas.

The rains had come just in time to stop a new wave of rationing
in the south-west. Five areas of Devon, including Exeter and
Plymouth, which were under threat of rationing, were given the
all-clear. It became possible, too, for the first steps to be taken to
restore supplies to those already rationed. About a fifth of the one
million people who since early August had had their supplies cut
off for seventeen hours a day now had their water restored. Their
supplies had been drawn from smaller reservoirs which had filled
quickly. Other people had the ban to their homes lessened, and
had to endure only a fourteen-hour rather than a seventeen-hour
stoppage. But the bigger reservoirs filled more slowly. By the end
of September, despite the rain, the north-west was said to be
down to sixty-nine days' supply. More water would have to be
drawn from Lake Windermere and from Ullswater, despite local
protests. In north Devon stand-pipes were still in use, and indeed
a further 60000 people in the area were warned that they might
have to go over to stand-pipes within the next few weeks, despite
the continuing rain.

But people had had enough. If the Government was not ready
to gamble on the rains continuing, the public were. A clamour
arose for the mains to be switched on again. Housewives were not
prepared to queue in the rain to draw water from stand-pipes.
The authorities waited a few more days, and then on 2 October
stand-pipe rationing ended officially.

At the same time an official assurance reached Leominster's MP
Mr Peter Temple-Morris. He was told that he could be sure that
farmers would get priority in supplies – but, the authorities added
cautiously, it would of course be difficult to get a supply to every
farmer in need. We added this assurance to our list of the drought's
ironies. A week later we received full permission from the Water
Authority to go onto the mains. We sat down, and did our sums
again. A further factor had now arisen. Our neighbour had already
planted the field across which the pipe would have to run. He
would need compensation for any damage done to his crop. But
the chief factor was the basic cost. We had sold our cattle at a
better price than we had dared hope, but well below what they
would have brought in a normal year. The margin of profit by
which we could have paid for the installation of the mains water

had disappeared. We had no choice but to file away the permission, and prepare to gamble on our own supplies again. We had survived – but the price of survival was that we had to accept for at least one more year the risk that the drought would strike again.

14. Aftermath

The Great Drought ended officially on 8 October. That was the day on which the Department of the Environment announced that it was over. The rationed areas came back onto the mains. The stand-pipes were removed, but carefully stored against another non-rainy day. By 12 November the last of the restrictions imposed by the major water authorities had been lifted. The last to go in these major areas were bans on hose-pipes in the Thames area, and around Eastbourne and mid-Sussex. A few small pockets of the country were still affected by minor curbs, but virtually the whole country was back to normal. Understandably enough, the authorities announced that they were only suspending their restrictions, not abandoning them. It was not until the driest summer for 200 years was followed by the wettest winter since records began that the Government began to speak with any confidence of the prospects for 1977.

The drought was estimated to have added £35 million to the cost of providing Britain with its daily water supply. This included £300000 for the 'Save Water' advertising campaign in September, launched when the rains were already under way. Much of the cost would find its way through to the public in the form of higher water rates. These were likely to increase by 20 per cent in 1977. The first rates increases came through early in the year. In Herefordshire farmers and other metered users would have to pay 64p per thousand gallons – an increase of 8p. The water authorities reckoned they would be spending some £185 million in Britain as a whole on improving supplies for the future.

Some lessons had been learnt. In October Lord Nugent, chairman of the National Water Council, presented the report the

Government had called for when the drought was at its height. He looked forward with some confidence. Even if there was another drought in 1977, supplies would be better. Even if the winter proved dry, a 'combination of urgent action by the water industry and careful use of water by consumers will put us in a sound position by next spring'. Pipelines were being laid from areas of likely surplus to areas of likely shortage; more water would be taken from rivers; new bore-holes would be sunk, and others deepened.

The basic policy of the Government and of the water authorities had been to gamble on getting through the drought without taking any really drastic steps, and no doubt they could say that their gamble had been successful. For one thing, it was clear that any such steps would have to be drastic indeed. The Great Drought had taught one lesson − that water is by no means an easy substance to move from one area to another. Such huge quantities of it are needed that anything like a water grid would be astronomically expensive. Other ideas for the bulk transport of water, whether in ocean-going tanker vessels or − as one scientist proposed − in huge plastic containers dragged behind barges, raise almost as many problems as they solve. Such supplies have to be pumped into storage reservoirs from the quayside − and pipelines and pumping systems do not exist for this. Other imaginative ideas like changing or reversing the flow of rivers might have done more harm than good by destroying the whole system of life and growth that depended on the rivers being as they are. Certainly every angler in the country heard of these suggestions with horror. So in the end the Government could no doubt congratulate itself on having relied on the British weather to come to its aid − as it did. But the very real hardships which a policy of rationing and wait-and-see had imposed upon millions of people will remain graven into the memories of all of us who were caught up in this struggle.

Recriminations about official policy began to fly before it was clear that the drought was really over. *The Times* in October argued that in some areas restrictions were imposed later than was sensible because the authorities did not want to have an outcry that water, having just been made more costly, had also been made immediately more scarce. The authorities wanted time for the memory of higher water rates to die away before they cut back supplies. In other areas water had been plentiful, but the pressure of public opinion had led the authorities to impose quite unnecessary restrictions. And where action had been taken, it was often too little and too late. Certainly if ever there was a crisis which had been solved by the time-honoured British tradition of muddling through, the water crisis of 1976 was one. If there is one message which those of us who experienced the drought at firsthand would preach for the future it is – act early. Impose savings before the reservoirs get too low. Because a gamble may not pay off a second time.

The effects of the drought stayed with Britain far into the long wet winter. Fresh vegetable prices, as everyone predicted back in the summer, reached hitherto unattainable heights. Cauliflowers were thought cheap at 45p each, brussels sprouts were 34p a pound, cabbage and other winter greens as much as 25p a pound, carrots 18p, onions 18p. Even the humble swede was hard to find at 12p a pound. Potatoes, at between 12p and 16p a pound, were in danger of losing their place as an essential constituent in the traditional pattern of 'meat and two veg' on the country's dinner table.

This reflected in money terms the shortfall in farm crops caused by the drought. The National Farmers' Union estimated that the parched fields had yielded two million tons less wheat and barley than would have otherwise been produced; that the potato crop was down by some two to two and a quarter million tons; that the loss of sugar beet had been higher still, perhaps as high as two and a half million tons; and that the country's cows had produced well over 100 million fewer gallons of milk. Though crops had been harvested earlier than usual, and though they had been gathered in more easily, with less damage from rain, they were appreciably lighter in yield.

The housewife did not stop to attribute these increases to the drought. They were lost in the general surge of inflation. Still less did she have occasion to take note of the degree to which farmers had been hit by the long dry months. When the official figures came out, and it was shown that farm incomes for 1976 were down 9 per cent in real terms – a greater cut than that experienced by anyone else except the unemployed and those on fixed incomes – the news hit no headlines except in the farm journals. Besides townspeople had other things to think about. For one thing the drought had struck at the foundations of thousands of houses. As the soil had dried out, particularly in areas of clay, it had cracked and separated, causing damage and subsidence to the houses that it supported. The British Insurance Association estimated that between £50 million and £60 million was paid out for subsidence claims for 1976. Not all the damage, of course, could be attributed to the drought, but there is no doubt that the dry weather caused a substantial amount of it.

But at least we did not have to face a hazard which the drought had exposed in northern France. The dust and crumbling soil there had yielded up unexploded shells which had been entombed for sixty years deep in what had been the mud of World War I.

Lashing and incessant rain in the winter of 1976–7 brought more subsidence problems, particularly to minor roads. (Even the rain, we were told, was a consequence of the drought. Meteorologists explained that abnormally high sea temperatures in September had caused more water to be taken up into the atmosphere.)

Around us in Herefordshire the country lanes were pitted with pot-holes and in places they were ankle-deep in mud from minor landslides as adjoining banks collapsed into the road. Our own farm drive was badly affected. Most of the surface of Rock Bottom Lane, the stretch leading from the village, was washed away in the heavy September thunderstorms. With more restricted resources than the county council we were forced to repair our own exclusive half-mile stretch with any materials available.

Houses can be shored up, roads can be resurfaced. But the drought damage to Britain's wildlife is less easy to repair and is likely to be with us for many years. Some animals, like rabbits, continued to thrive in the dry conditions. By 1977 their numbers had increased to such an extent that they were again posing a threat to farm crops. Farmers were urged to revive the Rabbit Clearance Societies, disbanded five years before when it looked as though myxomatosis had wiped most of them out for ever. With four out of every five rabbits now recovering from the disease and gaining immunity to it, and being further helped by mild winters they are breeding successfully throughout the whole year.

For most animals, particularly those we encourage to breed, it was a different story. Fish died in their thousands because of high temperatures, low river levels and, in tidal waters, because of critically low concentrations of dissolved oxygen. On the River

Wye, for instance, dissolved oxygen was severely depleted by increased weed growth and subsequent decomposition. The effects of the drought were particularly serious where salmon and trout fisheries were concerned. In many rivers salmon were unable to ascend weirs and obstructions because of low river flows. Those which did manage the journey upstream often found that the minor tributaries they traditionally use as spawning grounds had dried up completely. On most southern rivers the rod catches for the season were less than half the average for a normal year. One group of fishing folk, though, had a bumper year – the poachers. The drought provided ideal conditions for them to practise their skills since many fish were stranded in sea pools, waiting for the high flows that never came.

Coarse fisheries fared better and the effect on future fishing is thought to be less bleak than for salmon and trout. Nevertheless many thousands of fish died from high temperatures and low dissolved-oxygen levels, despite a huge effort by water authorities staff to transfer hundreds of thousands of endangered fish to other waters. Oddly enough, though, in one or two places the drought actually improved fishing. On the lower River Severn, below Tewkesbury, the movement of large numbers of coarse fish downstream from the middle reaches meant there was a period of excellent fishing.

The long hot summer also took its toll of birdlife. Robins and blackbirds were the main victims because their main source of food, the earthworm, was in short supply. The worms were forced deep into the dry hard ground well out of range of any hungry beaks. But other birds, like song thrushes and chaffinches, disappeared from Britain's back gardens in the spring of 1977 for a different reason. There was an abundance of natural foods available because of the mild winter and they found it unnecessary to rely on man's generosity. In general, despite the lack of robins and blackbirds, ornithologists have no real fears for the future of Britain's birdlife. By 1977 there were more varieties of birds nesting in Britain than at any time since records began.

It is difficult for anyone to avoid seeing the most devastating effect of the Great Drought on Britain's countryside. Trees are dying in their thousands. Many were dead before the heat-wave came to an end. Silver birches succumbed to a fungus, saplings and broad-leafed trees growing in shallow soils died from straight lack of moisture. A mature tree, after all, needs 200 gallons of water a day. But the real extent of the damage did not show up until the spring of 1977. As the grass came back underfoot many thousands of trees struggled into leaf for what was to be their last season. The shortage of water had robbed older trees of the strength necessary to combat disease. The Forestry Commission likened the effects to a flu epidemic among older people. What a young person may shrug off can be fatal to the very old. The main trees affected are beeches and sycamores – beeches are being attacked by beech bark disease while sycamores are battling with sooty bark disease. In the New Forest alone 8000 mature beeches and sycamores have died.

The hot dry summer also intensified the spread of dutch elm disease. The beetle that spreads the disease does not take wing until the temperature reaches about 60 degrees F. In 1975 and 1976 there were months and months on end when this critical temperature was reached. In warm weather too the beetle may breed twice in a season.

It is now estimated that in the southern half of Britain, below a line drawn from the Humber to the Mersey, half of all the elm trees are dead. The other half of the country remains threatened. In the north and Scotland, where there are fewer elms, some 25 per cent of them are affected. But a few may survive the plague – those isolated trees out of range of the beetle.

Some of the beeches and sycamores that appear to be dying off from the top of their branches stand a good chance of recovering. But it is likely that a chilling reminder of the Great Drought will remain etched on the skyline of southern Britain for many years.

The drought also left some hazards to human health. One was a dangerous increase in the nitrate levels in the water. In East Anglia in particular the nitrate levels had built up, in part from the artificial fertilizers spread on the fields and not absorbed by the soil. This had washed into the reservoirs. The Water Authority began stockpiling pure bottled water for babies.

But the drought was also a life-saver. 1976 saw the most dramatic drop in baby deaths in England and Wales for more than twenty years. For each 1000 live births there were only 13.9 deaths in children under one year old, compared with 15.7 in 1975. The drop equalled the combined fall over the previous four years. There was also a sharp fall in the death rate of babies after the first week of life. This dropped by as much as 25 per cent in the months of July, August and September 1976. The Office of Population Census attributed this to the fine weather of the summer, following upon a mild winter. Nature has indeed its own way of balancing things up.

I started to write this account of the Great Drought in the long still evenings when Tom was collecting water from the Hopkinses' supply. We had no idea at the time when the rain would come – or indeed if it ever would.

Was it the beginning of the end of life in Britain as we had always known it? There were times that summer when that seemed a real possibility. We had to gird our minds to the possibility that a long hot summer would be followed by a long dry autumn, and by another waterless winter, leading to a 1977 as arid and hostile as 1976 was proving to be. We hardly dared dream of life returning to normal, of having mud under our feet instead of dust swirling into our eyes, of seeing again the familiar and much-loved surroundings of a green and thriving countryside. I found myself thinking with longing of the days when the washing was just thrown into the machine, when baths were a delight to look forward to at the end of a long hard day, when to remove the jam which the baby had smeared on his face I needed only to rinse a cloth under a running tap

Had the drought not broken, the winter would have been for millions of people a period of extraordinary hardship. We would have suffered on our isolated farm, but many others would have been drawn into acute suffering. People would have had to trudge in the bitter cold of winter to collect their water from stand-pipes. Tap water would have become increasingly a forgotten dream, baths and flush lavatories would have seemed part of a vanished civilization. Large sectors of industry would have had to close down, many more people would have been thrown out of work.

The rains came in time to prevent all this, and came with such abundance that we were told we need have no worries for 1977. Yet there are voices raised to which anyone who felt the full force of the Great Drought is bound to listen with care. The Climatic Research Unit of the University of East Anglia is one of these. Dr Kelley, of this unit, told the East Anglian Planning Council in

September 1976 that we can no longer rely on summers with pre-
vailing southwesterly winds that bring in a sure supply of rain.
There has been a change in the wind circulation just south of the
Arctic. This is now more powerful, and more regular, with a result
that the rain-bearing depressions tend to move from the Atlantic
to the Arctic on a more northerly course than in the past, making
Scotland wetter and England drier. Dr Kelley's views, if I understand them rightly, are that the atmospheric circulation is what
conditions climate; that circulation has in its turn been affected
by the amount of dust thrown up into the upper atmosphere by
volcanic eruptions. Not only has volcanic activity increased since
1940, but the increasing pollution of the upper atmosphere by man
is now playing its part. We have therefore, he argues, to face the
fact that for some decades to come most summers in Britain – or
certainly in southern Britain – will be drier than we regard as
usual. The odds are no doubt against our having to face a second
summer drought of the same intensity as struck us in 1976, but it
seems sensible that we should work on the assumption that we
live in a country where summers will more often be dry than wet.

The official view on the drought was more comforting. In its
annual report for 1976 the Meteorological Office concluded that
the drought and the waterlogged months that followed provided
a sequence of events that can be expected to occur only once in
500 years. The extremes of temperature and rainfall during that
two-year period did not suggest a big or permanent change in the
British climate.

Farmers have, like sailors, always lived in intimate contact with
the weather. For them the weather forecast is the central item in
the news. The drought made farmers' wives as acutely conscious
of weather changes and of weather prospects. It struck right into
our homes, into every corner of our lives.

We had a glimpse of doomsday in 1976, and it stays in our
minds, however reassuring – indeed however exasperating – have
been the pounding rains and high winds of winter.

Life goes on as it always did – almost. When we dig holes for
fence posts we see that the earth is still bone-hard only three feet
under its topping of mud. We plan for the summer ahead on the
assumption that it will be hot and dry, and are cutting down our
beef herd – even if that means cutting down on our chances of
piling up enough funds to get on the mains at long last.

But it is a new year, and there are new problems. The ground is too soft to muck out the cattle sheds and spread the manure on the fields. The floor level in the sheds is rising, which makes the cattle nice and warm, but delays the time when we can get out onto the open ground that manure of which, as John Hopkins once remarked, 'beef is a by-product'. Autumn-sown corn has rotted in the waterlogged ground; potatoes and sugar beet remain unharvested.

So we move towards another season, with its new problems – and with some of the old problems still with us. As we drive through Micklebury we see the retired postman pumping water into a chipped enamel bucket from the village well. Further out into the country, a white-haired woman stoops by a ditch to fill a jug with water from a pipe sticking out from the bank. That is one corner of Britain in 1977.

Appendix A

The water we use each day

Average use per person*	_gals_
WC flushing and garbage-grinding	12·5
personal washing and bathing	12·5
laundering	3·5
dishwashing and cleaning	3·5
gardening	1·5
drinking and cooking	1
car-washing	0·5
TOTAL	35

Average use on the farm	
each cow (drinking, cleaning equipment, milking parlour, etc.)	20+
each bullock	2–12

Water used by each operation	
flushing WC	2
automatic washing machine	40
bath	30
shower	5
washing-up (meal for four)	5
hose-pipe on for one hour	200+

* SOURCE: Thames Water Authority

The 1976 rainfall deficit in Herefordshire

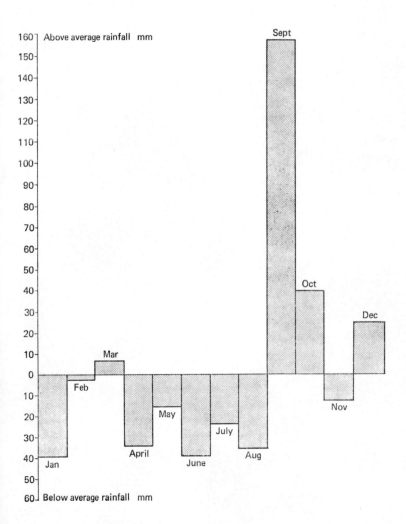